Modern Buddhism

by the same authors

A MEDITATION RETREAT

JACQUI AND ALAN JAMES are Buddhist meditation teachers who teach more than just 'how to meditate'. They give comprehensive guidelines for the most effective way of living to support the spiritual search. Their teachings are uncluttered by religious rituals and provide a means whereby the sincere, hard-working meditator can make great strides forward on the spiritual path. With fifteen years of experience in teaching Westerners, they bring to life the ancient message of the Buddha in a way perfectly suited to modern men and women.

Since 1980, they have taught at The House of Inner Tranquillity, a retreat centre which they founded in Wiltshire, England. Here they regularly conduct residential courses in meditation, give lectures and evening classes, and spend many hours providing one-to-one personal tuition in the Buddhist way.

In 1986 Jacqui and Alan founded The Monastery of Absolute Harmony which adjoins the retreat centre. This has provided the opportunity for male meditators to become monks and dedicate more of their time and energy to the spiritual path than is normally possible.

Today there are active plans for a separate extension to the Monastery to accommodate those female meditators who wish to become nuns.

The cost of publishing this book has been met entirely by donations from the following:

Carl and Sue Bishop
Joan and Bob Beckley
Paul MacRae
Rose Youd
Lin Quantick
Bodil Hart

The authors, proof reader, cover photographer and the directors of the publishing company have donated their services free in order that all the profits from the sale of this book can be given to the Aukana Trust, a registered Buddhist Charity, which has as one of its functions the support of the monks living in the Monastery of Absolute Harmony.

MODERN BUDDHISM

Jacqui & Alan James

AUKANA PUBLISHING
Ardgay House
Middlehill
Box
Wiltshire
England

© Aukana Trust 1987
First published in 1987 in Great Britain by
Aukana Publishing
Ardgay House, Middlehill, Box, Wiltshire, SN14 9QD.

Typeset in Times by
Saxon Printing Ltd, Derby
Printed in Great Britain by
A. Wheaton & Co. Ltd, Exeter
Cover photograph by Nigel Skene

British Library Cataloguing in Publication Data

James, Jacqui
    Modern Buddhism
    1. Buddhism—Doctrines
    I. Title II. James, Alan
    294.3'42   BQ4150

    ISBN 0−9511769−1−9

Contents

*This book is a collection of lectures
given by the authors
to their meditation students.*

The Buddha's Teaching
is not an
Alternative Therapy

Each of us has somehow to choose a direction in life. We have to choose what we want to work at; we have to select our own objectives and our own life-styles. The majority of people initially find it difficult to know what is most worthwhile. They try a bit of this, a bit of that; they try many different things, only to find that each is in some way lacking. They discover that the things they attempt are not quite what they had anticipated; that they are not really what they had wanted to do. Often they just drift into things, for want of any clear idea of what would be most fulfilling.

Many people leave school or, even later, university, having achieved good academic qualifications and still with absolutely no idea of what they really wish to do. Very often they have no idea why they took up history or geology or whatever it might be in the first place. To protest that 'it seemed a good idea at the time' begins to wear thin when your very livelihood is threatened by doubt and indecision.

Why do you think that it seems so difficult for some people to find a direction in life? Go back perhaps a hundred years and selecting a life-style was not the problem it seems to be today. A young man followed in dad's footsteps or took whatever was available. A young woman expected to get married, raise children and spend her life as a wife and mother. Today, these options seem to us to be too limiting;

1

we have come to expect more from life than our grandparents did. Paradoxically, the variety of choice seems to be growing smaller and smaller as we become more and more technologically sophisticated.

For many young people, the question of livelihood becomes increasingly urgent as hundreds of them chase one regular job. Are they destined to be a drain on the State from the age of sixteen or seventeen, perhaps indefinitely? How do we make sense out of a life in which the traditional work ethic has become an apparently impossible dream? How do we choose a direction?

The Unpleasant Facts
The Buddha's first noble truth states that suffering (*dukkha*) exists in the world. Suffering in this context does not mean only physical distress such as hunger and disease; it covers a much wider range. Suffering, grief, woe, lamentation and despair—all these are dukkha. Not knowing what you wish to do in life is very much an occasion for sorrow, for frustration, sometimes for grief and woe. It applies not only to jobs but also to every other aspect of life. Wherever there is dissatisfaction, however slight, that is suffering.

Nowhere is this more apparent than in relationships. Whether our relationships are sexual, platonic, deep or shallow, harmonious or bitter they are important to us and occupy a great deal of our time and mental involvement. We make relationships. We break them. In the process we get hurt. Being hurt, we wonder how to protect ourselves. Wondering how, we try to avoid the hurt or to avoid forming new relationships. Whatever we do, from time to time we experience dissatisfaction, we sorrow, we grieve. All of these things are dukkha. When we get hurt in any way, the temptation usually is to avoid what we consider to be the source of the problem. Perhaps we believe the problem to lie in relationships of a certain kind or perhaps in a certain kind of job. Perhaps we place the blame for our problems on the life-styles we lead or on the kinds of place in which we live.

Problems with the Environment

How often have you yourself said or heard it said by others: 'This job is boring. It's a job that could be done by a trained chimpanzee. It degrades human beings (never mind the chimpanzee!). I have to do it because it brings in the money but I don't really enjoy it.'

How many people have worked for someone who they thought to be unjust, ignorant and incompetent? Moaning about the boss is of course a favourite pastime but some people really believe that everything would come right if only they could have a different person in authority over them.

How often do a man and woman meet, form a relationship, get married and, after the first flush of enthusiasm has worn off, then come to believe that they have made a terrible mistake? The divorce statistics show that fewer and fewer couples are staying together for a long time. There is sorrow in the world, there is grief. There is woe, lamentation and despair. Divorce is always suffering.

Some people believe that everything would come right if they could change partners. Some people believe that everything would come right if only they could find the right job. Other people believe that everything would come right if only they could find the right place in which to live.

Take houses, for example. A brand new house has an enormous number of advantages: it has all the 'mod cons', all the right cupboard space and just about everything you might need. It is really well designed. It does not have much 'character', which some people consider to be a grave disadvantage and, from this point of view, the new house is dukkha, it is unsatisfactory. An older house may have all kinds of character—and rising damp, and woodworm, and frightening electrical wiring... You cannot have it all ways. Nothing is perfect. There is unsatisfactoriness in everything you can think of.

What is the solution? Is the solution to get rid of the

3

house, the job, the partner? I wonder. Let's pursue the theme.

The Real Causes of Distress

Why is it that relationships, houses, jobs and life-styles are unsatisfactory? Why is it that they are dukkha? The teaching of the Buddha gives a very simple answer: all these sufferings arise dependent upon craving and attachment. This statement is met with so often in the study of Buddhism that I am sure that it tends to lose its meaning for many people. Let us examine it more closely.

Suffering can arise upon fifty mental concomitants. A few of them are envy, jealousy, hatred, resentment, frustration, greed, ambition, selfishness and conceit. All these things are causes or major conditions for the arising of frustration and unhappiness. Every time you become envious of someone else's possessions or relationships you cause suffering, you bring it about. Every time you become conceited about your own abilities or your own possessions, your own group of friends or anything else, you create dukkha. You bring it into existence where it did not exist before. These mental factors are the major conditions upon which suffering arises. The outer circumstances are more or less incidental.

You have an image of yourself as you would wish to be and, if for whatever reason you fail to match up to that image, then suffering ensues. Why? Because of your craving for and attachment to the image. If you did not have that particular image, you could not suffer. If you had no craving for the image you could not suffer.

In every case the mental factors of conceit, pride, jealousy, selfishness and envy produce a state of affairs in which the major component is an intense feeling of discomfort. All of you know the feeling of wishing that the floor would open up and swallow you because you have said something stupid. All of you know the feeling of jealousy. All of you know the feeling of anger, of pride, of conceit.

They are all observable as the origin of dukkha—of woe, sorrow, lamentation and despair. It is not some esoteric mystery. These are observable facts.

The Buddha's teaching, now over two and a half thousand years old, is as pertinent and as relevant today as it ever has been. It describes in a straightforward way the facts of human life which are observable by anyone who cares to take the trouble to investigate.

The origin of suffering is *not* in the outside world. The origin of suffering is not in the partner, the house, the job, the environment, the government or taxation. The origin of the problem is not 'out there'. The origin of the problem of suffering is within yourself. The origin of the problem is always craving, which includes specific factors of mind such as jealousy, envy, resentment, greed, anger and so on. None of these things can exist unless there is an ignorance of the true state of affairs, unless there is an ignorance of what life is *really* like. None of these mental causes can exist unless there is an ignorance, literally *ignore-ance*, of the way in which mind really works.

Removing Suffering and Distress
You have to discover how things actually operate if you want to remove suffering and frustration. How do you remove dukkha? By removing its origin. You remove things like envy, frustration, intolerance, anger, pride, conceit and selfishness. For this to be possible, you have to come to see that each of these things is in turn dependent upon ignore-ance of the true facts of existence.

Every job of work—it does not matter what it is—has both its good and its bad points. Any job is at times deadly dull, repetitive and boring. If you search constantly for the perfect job which is never boring, you will be disappointed, for it is in truth never to be found. On the other hand, if you have realised the truth of the matter—that all jobs are at times boring—then immediately resentment of your own job

5

disappears, for you recognise that *any* other job is subject to boredom as well. Seeing the truth of the matter, many of these seemingly insoluble problems simply disappear.

Possessiveness or attachment is another origin of dukkha. Many believe that it is possible to own things and even people. With a careful look at the facts it becomes obvious that we can never own anything, least of all another person because, even if we can 'hold on to them' for ten, twenty or thirty years, they are going to die in the end. It is impossible to possess anything or anyone. If that is truly seen, in every detail, then possessiveness *has* to disappear. It cannot exist in the light of the knowledge that possessiveness is actually impossible, that all things disappear, all things change, not in fact year by year but, if you see it clearly, instant by instant.

It is possible to come to the complete eradication of sorrow, grief, woe, lamentation and despair. It is possible to come to complete eradication of frustration and dissatisfaction. How? Not by getting rid of the boss or putting poison in somebody's cup of tea; not by moving house or by going to live in a hotter climate; not by changing jobs; not by getting a bigger car; not by having a broader circle of friends; not by having special or unusual relationships; not by becoming better educated. None of these things help at all because they do not tackle the real problem.

The only way to remove dukkha is to remove its origin. The origin of suffering is craving and attachment in the form of pride, conceit, envy and so on. All these things are based upon an ignore-ance of the true facts of life. Thus the way to eradicate all of these causes of suffering is by removing ignore-ance by deliberately setting out to apply attention to things as they really are.

It is possible, here and now in the twentieth century, to eradicate ignore-ance totally and to come to the total cessation of suffering. It is not a long-lost secret enshrined in the tales of the past. It is not something magical or mystical which can be approached only through myth and fable. It is something real and something that, given the right approach and the right attitudes, anyone can realise in this modern day and age and in these technological conditions. Enlightenment, the cessation of suffering, is not something out of reach. It is absolutely real and ever-present and its discovery rests solely upon reversing the trend of ignore-ance with which each individual has been conditioned and with which he has conditioned himself. In reversing that trend anyone can come to see things as they truly are. Then there is a transcendence of such things as conceit, selfishness, envy, jealousy, pride and frustration; none of these things exists any more, and life is smoother and the more beautiful for it.

Alternative Life-Styles

You choose a direction in life based upon the many facets of your own character and on the many different beliefs you hold. You choose a way of life from amongst the available opportunities on the one hand but conditioned by your own hopes, beliefs and aspirations on the other. People are taught today that to be well off financially, to be well housed, to be well educated and to be healthy are perhaps the most that anyone can expect and that, given those things, they will be happy. It does not of course work like that, as you know. You can have a superb job, a lovely house, 2.4 children and all the trappings of success and still be desperately unhappy even though, as the saying goes, you do suffer in comfort.

A happy life does not rest on material success. Perhaps the recognition of this fact is one reason why there are so many recreational centres springing up across the country. For example, over the last decade or so sports centres have become very much more prominent than ever they were, which could be a sign of increasing affluence but equally could be a sign that people recognise that there is more to life than just working, eating and paying off the mortgage.

There do need to be concerns other than material. Interest is growing in what were once described as fringe

7

activities or alternative life-styles. There is a growing acceptance of once mistrusted activities like hypnotherapy and hypnosis, acupuncture and acupressure. All kinds of alternative therapies are beginning to come very much into prominence. If you ever go to the Psychics and Mystics Fair, take a look round the various stalls and displays. There is a wealth of interests to choose from.

There are many, many alternative therapies. What are their objectives? What are they designed to do? The advocates of all these 'new' things tell you that they are going to improve the quality of your life in some way. They are going to make life happier and more rewarding for you. They claim to fulfil your untapped potentials in a number of different directions. 'Take up flower arranging and unleash your creative potential.' Or, 'Take up yoga, remove stress and enjoy life more.' All have essentially the same message: '*This* will improve the quality of your life.'

Buddhism and Alternative Therapies
At the same time as popular awareness of alternative therapies is growing so too is interest in Oriental philosophy and religion. Since the turn of the century there has been a great upsurge of interest in the spiritual paths of the East, perhaps to offset the distinctly materialistic bias of our own culture. Many people have made the acquaintance of some form of meditation or mental discipline and have found it to help in alleviating some of their problems. There is, however, an attendant danger with the kind of superficial meeting of two cultures that occurs on the popular front: deep and subtle teachings are not fully understood and there is often serious misunderstanding and corruption of ancient truths.

You can see strong evidence of this today in certain circles. Some people maintain that at the very heart of Buddha Dhamma, the teaching of the Buddha, lies nothing more nor less than a simple relaxation technique designed to enable you to cope better with your life. They view these

8

pristine teachings as a rather over-complicated manual for the relief of stress in day-to-day living. Under this heading, too, comes the practice of meditation: it is seen as an effective method of normalising your responses to daily crises and to the pressures of modern living.

There are psychiatrists and psychologists who today teach 'meditation' to their clients. Many alternative therapists proclaim the benefits of 'mindfulness', as they see it. Many a practitioner teaches 'awareness' and, learning that the way of the Buddha is founded on the development of awareness, comes to the conclusion that they are talking about the self-same thing.

The adoption of terminology from ancient teachings is of dubious benefit to the therapist and is extremely damaging to people's understanding of the ancient ways themselves. It is not a new problem and perhaps the problem is not so severe as sometimes it seems, for those who are truly seeking the right path to understanding will never be fooled for long by imitations.

The great majority of practitioners of alternative therapies act always from the best and purest of motives, wishing only to help people where they can and by whatever means seem to them to be true and effective. There is no suggestion that alternative therapies are deliberately and consciously mis-representing Oriental teachings such as Buddhism. It is true, however, that most of them are unaware of the scope and range of the age-old teachings.

The crux of the matter is that the aims of alternative therapies fall far short of the aim of Buddha Dhamma. If they would claim otherwise they would be mistaken, for they are not directed towards and have no teachings for the control and eradication of ignorance, desire and attachment. To this extent Buddhism can in no way be classified as an alternative therapy as some would claim. It is in a class of its own.

The primary aim of the teaching of the Buddha is not to improve the 'quality of life'. The prime objective of

Dhamma is to come to enlightenment which is the transcendence of all opposites. To become enlightened is to have removed utterly all desire for and attachment to pleasure and pain, to gain and loss, to fame and obscurity, to praise and blame. In other words, the enlightened individual is *not concerned* if he experiences pain or pleasure. He or she is not concerned if a cycle of loss starts to make itself felt. He or she is not elated if things are going particularly well nor depressed if things are going badly.

None of the therapies is a way to enlightenment. The two words do not belong in the same sentence; there is no connection between them. The various therapies may be perfect for relaxing you, for giving you a buzz for the time being and for smoothing away the stresses and strains of the day; they may be ideal for alleviating the symptoms associated with conditions such as arthritis. There is no way in the world that they can reduce the central originating factor of suffering. They do not reduce or remove ignorance and its associated craving and attachment.

The whole point of the Buddhist teaching is to develop for yourself the skills to overcome suffering and not to go to someone else who does it to you or for you. It can be done only by each individual for himself, by himself—admittedly under very necessary guidance, but the individual has to be the one who does it. Only the individual is able to remove the scales of ignorance from his own eyes. Only the individual can control and eradicate his own desire and attachment. It is not possible for a teacher somehow to transfer to another the fruits of his or her own past labours to eliminate ignorance and attachment. The student has to do it personally. A teacher can only suggest a line of enquiry or a direction of endeavour. A teacher can only point the way, urging the individual student to work hard for his own personal benefit and for that of others. The question of finding a direction in life becomes of particular importance when we consider spiritual development.

The Most Profitable Way to Live
It's not so much what you do that is important; it is rather the way that you do it. The perfect direction in life is to develop an enquiring attitude into everything. To have an enquiring attitude means to pay attention to whatever you do or to the circumstances into which you fall, with an eye which is as far as possible unjaundiced and unbiased. You want to see precisely what *is* taking place; to see precisely how emotional states arise and pass away; to see exactly how it is that woe, sorrow, lamentation and despair are born in the mind.

How many people here have been depressed? Right. Everybody has been depressed. Some of you might be depressed right now. Why? How? How did it come to be? If you are intent on trying to observe, you will find out and you will also see how the other aspects of suffering arise. You will see how depression comes into existence and, seeing, you will recognise that it arises because there is selfishness in the mind. You want something for yourself which for one reason or another you cannot get. There is a frustrated craving or attachment based on a refusal to face facts. You cling to an unreasonable expectation and try to achieve something which is in fact impossible.

The essential thing is to recognise that if one takes as a direction in life the development of an attitude of watchfulness, then that attitude will be present no matter what you choose to do with your life—whether you are employed or whether you are not; whether you have a house or whether you do not; whether you have a relationship or whether you do not; whether the relationship you do have is happy or miserable. To develop an attitude of attentiveness or watchfulness with the idea of discovering truly how mind works is something which is possible in every life-style, in every life circumstance, and its rewards are incalculable. It is possible for life to be fulfilling all the time for each individual human being, independently of material gain and loss, or of emotional satisfaction or desolation.

11

Religion and the Way to Transcendence

The attitude of constant enquiry and watchfulness contrasts markedly with the practice of the forms of religion. Religion in this sense is the ritualisation of something that happened a long, long time ago. Buddh-ism is a religion of this kind and differs markedly from the teaching of the Buddha. Buddhism consists of a collection of rituals built upon the memory of the enlightenment of one man over two and a half thousand years ago. Those rituals are enacted in temples (churches) in the belief that somehow they bring one closer to the highest of which man is capable.

The best description of a ritual I can give you is as follows. A friend of ours had a house in which all the doors swung closed by themselves after they had been opened. When he went from the living room into the kitchen to get some tea he would prop the door open with a pouffe, carry the tea back into the living room on a tray and then remove the pouffe to allow the door to swing closed. His young grandson had seen this done many times and so, whenever he wanted to go into the kitchen, he would open the door, move the pouffe, and walk out through the door—which would swing shut behind him. He had learned the sequence of events but had not realised that the pouffe had to be in contact with the door. There he was religiously—and I use the word advisedly—moving the pouffe toward the door every time he wanted to go out, not recognising what it was for.

That is a ritual. You do not understand why you are doing it but you do it religiously. Does it help you? No, the door still shuts. What we want to do is open the door and keep it open. The only way you do that is with intelligence and that means using an intelligent watchfulness all the time. As soon as you descend into ritual you are blind because you have put your faith and trust in something which you do not understand and which is probably not formulated in a meaningful way anyway. Ritualists lose themselves in their rituals; they do not intend to learn anything from them.

The rituals of a religion contrast strongly with the truly effective ways of coming to see the truth on which they were originally based. If you have the patience and the perseverance to delve behind the rituals of any religious way, you will find effective techniques for the control of desire and attachment and the eradication of ignorance. Different methods suit different people but, for many, the teaching of the Buddha, as distinct from Buddh-ism, is a perfect way to come to see the truth.

Each person committed to the eradication of suffering and frustration has to develop an intelligent watchfulness in everything they do. It is only that which will reverse ignore-ance of the way in which desire and attachment cause all the distress in the universe. If you remove ignorance you remove attachment, you remove craving, and you remove hatred, envy, jealousy, possessiveness, selfishness, conceit, pride and all of that host of things upon which sorrow, woe, grief, lamentation and despair arise. Your freedom and enlightenment are, in the end, your own responsibility.

Spirituality

Spirituality is a word one rarely finds in connection with Buddhism. This is understandable because no mention is ever made in this teaching of things like 'Spirit' or 'Soul' or 'God', and one does tend to associate the word spirituality with religious ways that talk about the existence of a 'God' and a 'Soul'.

I want to talk to you about religion, mysticism, and spirituality and what I mean by these terms. I want to show you whether they do or do not fit in with Buddha Dhamma, the teaching of the Buddha, and I want also to talk to you about the magic of living in the moment and the ordinariness of living in the moment which come from true meditation.

What is Religion?
Firstly let's take a look at religion. To me, religion is all about a God out there, who is separate and different from human beings, and who imposes laws as to how man should live if he wishes to have a happy life once he leaves this earthly realm.

God's servants, the priests, ensure that God's followers keep his laws. Those laws are mainly to do with morals. So a priest's life is concerned with guiding his flock towards a more moralistic life-style. The more moral the life-style, the happier the person will be. That is the religious teaching.

The priest's life is also full of ritual and social welfare. He is involved in such activities as visiting the sick, conducting marriages, christenings and funerals, comforting the dying, and generally giving advice to his parishioners on how best to deal with these major turning points in their lives.

A priest may also get involved in issues like poverty, racial discrimination and nuclear disarmament that affect a portion of society larger than just his parish. There's many a priest in South America who spends much time and energy fighting for the down-trodden, and who opposes any political system which maintains the gap between the rich and the poor. These priests fight for justice and for the uplifting of humanity through political and social change.

Some priests are missionaries in third world countries. They encourage their former parishioners back in Ireland or Scotland to send them money, clothes, books, pencils, writing-pads and anything else which will help to alleviate the suffering of the people amongst whom they now work.

What is Mysticism?
Mysticism is quite different from religion. It is not at all concerned with social and political issues. It is not concerned with moral laws and getting others to follow those laws. It is not concerned with the poor, with the dying, with marriages and deaths. It is not concerned with chatting with parishioners.

The mystic is concerned only with a direct experience of God and, according to the mystic's religious background, he will call that direct experience 'God' or 'Brahma' or 'Reality' (with a capital 'R') or 'Nibbana'. Mystics are to be found in Buddhism, Hinduism, Christianity, Sufism and also outside of these formal religious groupings.

What the mystic understands by the word God is quite different from what the average religious man or woman in the street understands by this term. To the religious person, God is outside of himself. God rewards and punishes. To the mystic, God is within. God is not outside and separate from himself. To the mystic it is possible to have the direct experience of God in this very lifetime.

Mystics are contemplative by nature. They are drawn to organisations that spend much time in silence. They are drawn to silent monasteries, to retreat houses, to meditation centres. They are drawn to teachers who instruct them to be silent and to turn within. They are drawn to teachings which tell them that the answers lie within; that God lies within and can only be experienced when the mind has been stilled and quietened. Through the practice of silent contemplation the mystic attempts to lessen the obstacles that stand between him and God even though he knows that, in the final analysis, he must abandon himself totally and stop 'doing' anything in order to have that direct experience.

Mystics are happy to put into practice moral laws, and to serve humanity by teaching school or working amongst the poor, just so long as these activities reduce selfishness and thus get them that much closer to the direct experience of God for which they hunger. Should caring for others' welfare take up so much of his day that there is little time for contemplation, the mystic is no longer happy. For then life becomes crowded with social, religious and political matters and moves away from the inner, contemplative arena where he knows the answers lie.

What is Spirituality?
How does spirituality fit into the picture? Well, spirituality is really mysticism. The spiritual person hungers for the direct experience of Reality in this very lifetime. The spiritual person, like the mystic, is a contemplative by nature.

The only aspect of religion that the spiritual person is concerned with is that of morals, recognising that a good moral standard quietens the mind and is a necessary foundation on which to build the meditative life. The spiritual person knows, however, that a moral life is only the beginning and not the end of the spiritual journey. It is but one aspect of the endeavour, not the whole task.

A person who is utterly dedicated to becoming enlightened in this very lifetime is the only truly spiritual person. Such a person will, most definitely, meditate. The type of meditation he will do will be insight meditation even though it may be called by some other name in the particular way he is following.

The Spiritual Person

A spiritual person will use every means at his or her disposal to break down the ego which stands in the way of that direct experience of Nibbana. They will train themselves to be ethical. They will train themselves to meditate and to serve and, with time, they will learn how to serve with the right attitude of mind—more of which later. Spiritual people also learn how to turn difficult life situations, like a troublesome marriage, into something from which they can grow spiritually rather than something which tears them to bits, leaving them bitter and resentful. The spiritual person also trains himself to give of his time and his possessions as yet another means of breaking down self-centredness.

Spirituality is a term that still has most of the right associations linked with it. It implies someone who seeks something beyond the world he experiences in everyday life.

In contrast, to say someone is religious suggests a person dressed in some strange sort of garb, like a habit, which is different from what you or I wear, and who engages in keeping moral laws, participates in rituals and does good works. It may carry overtones which suggest that the person is old, smelling of mothballs, and has 'taken religion', like taking out some sort of insurance policy, just to ensure that everything goes smoothly after death. Saying a person is 'religious' can mean something derogatory: it can mean that the individual is a 'goody-goody'—someone apparently concerned with mental and physical purity but who is actually repressed both emotionally and sexually.

A spiritual way breeds real men and real women, not people who are scared of their masculinity or femininity in the way that a sexually repressed person is. A person who is walking the spiritual path correctly will never be accused of being a goody-goody. He may be labelled many other things but never that.

The Spiritual Path
A way can correctly be called spiritual if it teaches that it is possible to have a direct experience of Reality in this lifetime and if it teaches its followers what practices to engage in in order to bring about such an experience.

There are teachers of Buddhism who teach a spiritual way. There are teachers of Buddhism who teach religion. There are teachers of Buddhist meditation who teach a mental therapy. Those who teach religion and therapy do not believe it is possible to experience Nibbana in this lifetime, so they present the teaching in such a way that their emphasis falls in the wrong place. The message that comes across from the way they present the teaching is that meditation is a mental 'relaxer and toner' which leaves the meditator feeling refreshed and better able to cope with the rigours of the day ahead. With such an approach you would do half an hour's meditation in the morning to start the day right, just as you would jog or do yoga for half an hour in the morning in order to start the day right. Then you would breakfast on bran and orange juice and you're really set up for the day! I trust you know which of these divisions we teach without me having to spell it out for you.

The Dangers of the Popular Approach
What really stimulated this lecture tonight was a book on meditation that we recently received for the library. The message contained in this book is that insight meditation (*vipassanā*) is a mental relaxation technique. It is not. Vipassana is much more than a relaxation skill. It is a means to an end: the direct experience of Reality.

There is grave danger that, as vipassana meditation gets more popular and teachers of it wish to appeal to more and

19

more people, it will be stripped of its Buddhist background so that it does not offend others of different religious persuasions who believe in a God and a soul and who find the no-soul (*anattā*) theory and the no-God aspect of Buddhism hard to take. As soon as the meditation is stripped of its Buddhist roots then only concepts like 'paying attention to the moment' and 'watching sounds come and go' can be used. Any of the views which are so central to the teaching, like the view of non-self, must be abandoned so as not to offend. The whole drive of the Buddhist teaching is that the stains in mind are only there because of our wrong views, one of which is the belief that a soul or self or an ego (*attā*) exists as a real entity. To directly experience Reality one has to wear away the three wrong views of self, non-change and non-suffering.

The Theory of No-Self
The *anattā* theory is really very simple. Don't read more into it than you need to, or you'll decide you just can't understand it. Soul, self, ego are different words for the same thing. The self is defined as something which is solid and never-changing, and which is lodged somewhere in one's mind or body. It is believed to be permanent.

When we meditate we discover that we cannot find anything which is permanent in mind or body. Everything changes. Our body changes. Our feelings change. Our moods change. Objects in mind change. Everything we look at within ourselves or outside of ourselves changes, and that change is dependent upon conditions. You just cannot find anything within mind or body which is solid, stable and never changes. The fact that everything does change, dependent upon conditions, is what the word *anattā* means.

Enlightened Masters
There was an American gentleman called Julian Johnson who I feel sure would fully approve both of my definition of spirituality and of the idea that one should be aiming to

develop spirituality in this life.

In the 1970s he wrote a book called *With a Great Master in India*. 'Master' was what he and others called his teacher, an Indian living in India whose path through to enlightenment was via the Sikh religion. Mr Johnson makes no secret of the fact that his teacher was enlightened. His teacher is now dead as, I think, is Mr Johnson himself.

As so often happens to enlightened teachers, the Master was rejected by orthodox Sikhs because their traditional teachings claim that there is no such thing as an enlightened teacher in this day and age. That which is held as the highest authority in the Sikh religion is not an enlightened person but rather a book of holy scriptures. No wonder orthodox Sikhs frowned upon Baba Sawan Singh, more fondly referred to as 'the Master' by his followers.

Julian Johnson is very forthright and attacks Buddhism strongly saying that it has a superior system in the eightfold path but, like Christianity, it is a lifeless husk because it lacks a living Master. As far as Mr Johnson is concerned any teaching is useless if it does not have an enlightened person teaching it. Even if the person who founded the religion was enlightened that is of no use. What is important is that the teacher sitting before you in the flesh is enlightened.

This idea, that a pupil can only become enlightened provided his teacher is enlightened, is very commonly held. I agree with Mr Johnson's views. There will be the exception to the rule but, on the whole, unless one's teacher is enlightened it is not possible for a spiritual person to become enlightened. Unenlightened teachers subtly misdirect their pupils—not intentionally, but out of ignorance of the way. How can they possibly direct someone to the top of the mountain if they themselves have never been there? Such teachers can only guess the path.

Mr Johnson is strongly critical of Christianity and Buddhism because, as far as he can see, both these religions cannot produce enlightened beings because they do not contain any enlightened teachers. I cannot speak for Christianity but he's wrong about Buddhism. It does contain enlightened teachers. He obviously just hadn't met one.

The copy of Mr Johnson's book that we have was printed in 1975. It is the 6th edition since the book first appeared in 1971. The book was reprinted six times in four years. The publishers had 3,000 copies printed for the 5th edition and 5,000 for the 6th. Clearly, there is a great thirst amongst spiritual seekers for contact with, or knowledge of, real Masters.

How Does a Person Grow Spiritually?
How does a person become more spiritual? A person becomes more spiritual in only one way and that is by becoming more aware. The more aware a person is of what is going on inside him, particularly with respect to his body, feelings, mental states, and mental objects, the more spiritual that person is. The more aware the person becomes of how much the body and mind change, how such a state of affairs is unsatisfactory and how it cannot be controlled, the more spiritual still does that person become. He or she is aware of all the little movements of mind and is very aware of pain and suffering. Being so sensitive to suffering he develops a burning desire to rid himself of it, which is another way of saying he hungers for release, he hungers for Nibbana.

Someone who is not very aware of what is going on internally is not aware, for example, when there is ill-will present in mind except when it has multiplied enormously and has become a raging hatred. Such a person, whether meditator or not, has blindness (*avijjā*) strong in his or her make-up. As he or she is not very aware, and therefore not very spiritual, he does not have a burning interest either in the spiritual journey or the teaching. He may have lots of enthusiasm about the teaching but there is a big gap between what he would like to become and what he is doing about it in the moment—in short, his practice is weak.

Such people do not have a burning desire to free

themselves from the grip of suffering because they are not aware that they do suffer. They are unaware of the cravings and hatreds that operate within them.

The Inner and Outer Mind
There are two levels to the mind: the inner and the outer. The outer is what the majority of people see. It consists of the balance of skills necessary to deal with the outside world. It is in a sense the image one presents to the world. The inner mind consists of the wisdom—or lack of it—which governs the individual's approach to the spiritual path. It is more subtle than the outer mind and initially more difficult to perceive.

The outer mind can be very competent in handling life. It may be very outgoing and not at all shy when in a group of people. It may be able to handle very well such things as personal finances and property and working for a living. Perhaps it can relate successfully to the solicitor, the boss and the children with the greatest of confidence and ease. Most would say that such a person is very 'together'. He would seem to have no problems and what curves life does throw at him he handles with such ease that he does not even regard such events as problems. Outwardly he is fine. He has no problems. His outer mind is very aware and it is because he is so clearly aware of external things that he can handle them and can produce continual order in these areas.

Inside it may be a very different story. The inner mind may be a mess. It may be all smashed up and confused and he doesn't even know it for he lacks awareness of his inner world. Lacking awareness, there is nothing he can do to bring order into his inner mind. Without awareness he can never get rid of internal suffering and he cannot make progress on the spiritual path.

As meditation teachers we look only at the inner mind when assessing whether a person is or is not progressing at meditation. The outer mind remains much the same throughout life but the inner mind can change beyond all recognition. It is the inner mind which is transformed and spiritualised.

What does becoming more aware achieve? Becoming more aware internally begins to inform the individual that certain kinds of mental behaviour are as pernicious to the inner mind as cyanide is to the body. It begins to show that things like extreme selfishness introduce such enormous distress into the inner mind that life becomes almost unbearable. It illuminates the fact that attitudes of hatred and lust carry with them an enormous price in the form of inner suffering. It begins to show that actions like criticism and ignore-ance are what we normally think of as the ego itself, and it allows us to learn how to change the inner mind so that it becomes harmonious and helpful, rather than harmful and dangerous. Inner awareness reduces the ego. It reduces self-centredness and selfishness. Ego, self-centredness, selfishness—they all mean the same thing. Selfishness is a stain in the mind. Mind without selfishness is pure. By becoming more aware, we aim at cleansing the mind of stains and returning to our true nature, which is pure mind.

Work as a Spiritual Discipline

I said there was only one way of making the mind more spiritual and that was by becoming more aware of what is going on inside one in order to reduce selfishness. There are other things that we can do to chip away at the stains—such things as giving, the study of Dhamma and service. All these help to wear down the ego.

Let's look at service for a moment. Everybody can practise service every day. Service is having the right attitude when doing work for others and everybody does work for someone other than themselves every day. The nine-year-old boy who clears the breakfast table for his mum can serve, provided he has the right mental attitude to the task. The mother cleaning out the toilet for the family can serve if she has the right attitude towards the cleaning. The father clearing out a blocked drain can serve provided he has the right attitude. The gardener picking up leaves in the middle of autumn can also serve.

It all depends upon one's mental attitude towards the work. Work can appear boring, pointless, even degrading if one has the wrong approach. If one has the right approach one can spiritualise work, transforming it into something quite different: one can transform it into service.

The right attitude is to do the work to the best of one's ability, keeping one's mind in the moment and on the task in hand. It is to regard the job as a gift to those around one: you are making their surroundings more orderly and beautiful. Even if you only clear a table it makes the house more orderly and beautiful for others.

To expect there to be a *point* to work other than this would be the wrong attitude. That means you want to achieve something in the future: you are grasping for satisfaction in the future. When that is there, you are dead to the moment. For example, let's say that you have been asked to mow the lawn. Perhaps the lawn looks perfectly short to you and you see no point whatsoever to mowing it. When engaged in this work with the wrong attitude you will be surly, full of ill-will, and wishing the time away. You are dead to the moment. It is impossible for you to learn from anything you are doing at that time. You have wasted an opportunity for correct meditative practice.

If you can mow that lawn with full attention, doing it beautifully, not missing a blade of grass, then you are mowing that lawn with love. Humans and non-humans alike will love you for your care and gentleness. You have given a gift. You have served others.

If you can mow that lawn with the same care both when the grass is long and needs mowing and when the grass is short and doesn't appear to you to need mowing, then it means that you have overcome the opposite views of worth and worthlessness, success and failure, praise and blame. It means you have come to realise that everything that you have to do in life is worth doing, that there does not have to be a *point* to it, or a reward at the end of the task, or even praise from another in order for you to mow the grass well.

The attitude that you have towards work will be exactly the same attitude that you take into the meditation. If you are attached to seeing a result when you work then you will be attached to seeing a result when you meditate and will get very frustrated if you have been meditating for years and can't see any startling results. You can't have one attitude towards work and then miraculously switch it off and have a different attitude when you meditate.

One of the first things a meditator must learn is to be unaffected by praise or blame, to be unaffected by success or failure. The meditator must learn to take both in his stride; to experience the pleasant feeling when he is praised but to move on, to let go of that feeling. That is being unaffected by praise. He must learn to experience the unpleasant feeling when blamed but to move on, to let go of that feeling. That way one is unaffected by blame.

The easiest place to learn to be balanced towards praise and blame, success and failure, is in the arena of work. Hardly a week will go by when someone won't either praise you or blame you for the job you're doing. If you can learn the right attitude towards work, you are chipping away at those stains in mind that prevent you from directly experiencing Reality.

The Magic of Living in the Moment
When journeying along the spiritual path one has to strike a balance between the ordinariness of being in the moment and watching sensory impressions, feelings and thoughts come and go, and the overwhelming magic of living in the moment.

When the magic is there you may be standing in the garden at one of those still periods of the day, dawn or dusk, absorbing the atmosphere, listening to the hush, feeling the grass beneath your feet, smelling the fragrance in the air from the flowers. Without warning, it happens. You're overcome with a sense of joy. You'd like to jump up and hug the sky and the trees and the flowers and everybody in the world. You are filled with love, with loving kindness, for everything and it wells up in you and courses through your body in great waves. This magic, this love for just being, comes when the mind stops.

When someone has an experience like this he may call it spiritual. It is so outside his day-to-day moods and experiences that he cannot help but call it sacred. Should that joy and love which fills the whole body and mind be accompanied by a brilliant, white circle of light, even more does the person think, 'This is God'. That circle of light may be small, about the size of a pinhead, or large, the size of a plate. It will appear on whatever one is looking at. If one is in the garden with one's eyes open, looking at a tree, then the light will hang amongst the leaves or settle on the bark of the tree. It appears, hangs for a moment, then disappears. Sometimes it's followed by another light, then another and another. Someone without adequate training is very likely to think that he has been visited by God or a Presence or that this experience is enlightenment itself.

Such a conclusion would be a mistake for this is quite an ordinary experience on the spiritual path. The mind is for a moment or two free from hindrances and there is a little bit more concentration around than normal. When these conditions are present then a globe of light is seen, whether one's eyes are open or closed, and joy fills the whole mind.

This experience is both magical and at the same time ordinary. It is ordinary because it is conditioned and therefore cannot last. The globe of light will fade. The joy will fade. It is ordinary because it indicates nothing more fantastic than the fact that for a few brief moments you are living in the present, that your mind is free of stains and is well concentrated. It is not God or the devas or the angels who have come to visit you. The feelings of love and well-being—the being in the moment—that is magic enough. There is no need to add anything extra in the way of a false religious interpretation to such a magical experience.

Birth and Death

Some modern students of Buddhism value highly the wonderful precision and depth of the Buddha's teaching but tend to believe that ethical discipline and meditation are two 'optional extras' which are nice to do if you have the time and the inclination, but which are not really important to the main teaching.

On his deathbed the Buddha said, 'Whatever person lives in accordance with the Dhamma, conducts himself dutifully, and acts righteously, it is he who respects, reverences, venerates, honours and reveres the Tathagata with the highest homage.'

To respect the memory of the Buddha in a meaningful fashion it is necessary to attempt to follow every aspect of his teaching and not just acknowledge intellectually its admittedly wonderful precision and depth. The practice of ethical discipline and meditation is an integral part of the study of Buddhism.

The Way of Practice
To live by the Dhamma it is necessary firstly to understand that it is designed for one aim only. The aim of the Dhamma, the teaching of the Buddha, is to come to the complete cessation of suffering; to end all pain, all longing, frustration and dissatisfaction.

The Buddha described this goal in a number of different ways depending on whom he was speaking to at the time. One of his favourite descriptions was of the cessation of suffering as the end of birth and death, the beyond of the Wheel of Samsara. Attaining enlightenment, you cut off forever death and (re)birth. You cut off forever attachment to the relative and limited, plunging deep into the absolute and unlimited, 'the unborn, uncreated and unbecome'. What is not born cannot die. Attaining enlightenment, you attain the deathless.

Life and Death
In the West, many people hold the view that we have only one life after which there is oblivion. They might extend this belief to say that they live on through their children in a purely material fashion but they cannot entertain the idea of *personal* survival of death, no matter what evidence is put before them.

Others believe in the personal survival of death, but that it takes place in a heaven or hell which is eternal. They believe that they only have one shot at life as we know it and then, when it ends, there is everlasting happiness or sorrow, depending on how you have lived.

Outside of these circles, there is a *lot* of evidence that we survive death, even if we just consider our own culture. If we care to consider in addition the evidence available from the East, then how anyone can doubt the existence of personal survival of death is a mystery and seems only to reflect the amazing capacity of the human mind to ignore things. All the evidence suggests (although cannot of course *prove*) that personal survival of death is something we all have to live with. Not only that but, having survived death, we find ourselves in conditions where we will die yet again—and again survive. In short dying and being born is an endless process, going on and on and on without end. In Oriental teachings and in the teaching of the Buddha this is called

Samsara, which literally means 'perpetual wandering', and it is seen as most unsatisfactory.

Planes of Existence

There are many planes of existence upon which it is possible to be reborn. They range from the highest heavens to the lowest hells with the human realm somewhere in the middle. Life in any of these locations is for a limited time only; there is no eternal existence at any level. We are born now here, now there, always moving on when the time is right and never able to settle in any place, no matter how humble, no matter how exalted. Always there is change. Always there is moving on. Always there is perpetual wandering, whether we like it or whether we do not. The pattern in not random but is governed by natural laws the operation of which can be seen even within one lifetime.

Actions and Results

How we behave in one life affects conditions in the next. If we work hard at praiseworthy actions, then the next life will be a 'better' one than the one we experience at the moment. If on the other hand we work hard at actions which are blameworthy, then the next life will be less fortunate than this one, and we will increase our personal burden of suffering.

Whatever kind of action we spend much time and effort on, it is that which greatly affects our future direction. This should not be a great mystery. Everybody knows that it takes much dedication and effort to become skilled—whether at 'good' action or at 'evil' action—and that one does not really reap any rewards until after that effort has been expended and the skills developed.

Let me give you some idea of the kind of results you might expect from different actions. These results may be seen in the life in which the particular behaviour pattern becomes established or they may be seen in a later one. In the latter case it often appears that the person is enjoying wealth and acclaim or illness and suffering 'by chance' unless the wider picture is taken into account.

Actions Which Promote Distress
The following actions produce painful results both for oneself and for other people. The personal outcome of each is listed.

KILLING leads to a short life, ill-health, constant grief and constant fear.

STEALING results in poverty, misery, disappointment and a livelihood dependent on others.

SEXUAL MISCONDUCT brings many enemies, undesirable wives and husbands and an unfavourable rebirth.

LYING leads to being subject to abusive speech and vilification, untrustworthiness and bad breath.

SLANDER gives rise to dissolution of friendship without sufficient cause.

HARSH SPEECH results in being detested by others though absolutely harmless and to having a harsh voice.

FRIVOLOUS TALK is the cause of speech which no one believes.

COVETOUSNESS causes non-fulfilment of one's wishes.

ILL-WILL brings about ugliness, manifold diseases and a detestable nature.

FALSE VIEW is the cause of base desires, lack of wisdom, chronic diseases and blameworthy ideas.

Actions Which Promote Health and Welfare
Certain actions, notably those which minimise selfishness, produce results of a very different kind. The following are actions which promote happiness and harmony.

GENEROSITY yields wealth.

MORALITY gives birth in noble families and in states of happiness.

MEDITATION leads to birth in realms of form and formless realms and helps to gain higher knowledge and emancipation.

TRANSFERENCE OF MERIT acts as a cause to live in abundance in future births.

REJOICING IN OTHERS' GOOD FORTUNE is productive of joy wherever one is born.

EXPOUNDING AND HEARING THE DHAMMA are both conducive to wisdom.

REVERENCE is the cause of noble parentage.

SERVICE produces a large following.

PRAISING OTHERS' GOOD WORKS results in getting praise oneself.

SEEKING THE THREE REFUGES results in the destruction of passions.

MINDFULNESS is conducive to diverse forms of happiness.

Constant Change

Throughout the cycle of births and deaths, the 'same individual' is constantly changing. There is no stasis anywhere or at any time. Always things change. Nothing ever stays the same. This 'self' that we place so much store by is merely a temporary grouping of skills and abilities, outlooks and attitudes, all of which are in process of changing. As experience succeeds experience, as year follows year, as life follows life, so do these abilities and attitudes change, modified by experience and desire into something else. Truly there is no stability to be found in Samsara.

Some people find this idea uncomfortable. They want to cling to the gains they have already established. Others see instead immense possibilities for the future for, if everything is truly in a process of flux, then it is possible to change in whatever direction you desire. Life can improve in whatever way you wish it to, given enough time and application.

This is the truer picture. With enough time and dedication it is possible to remove certain defects of character and experience happiness and freedom almost impossible to imagine before. I know one meditator in particular who used to suffer from terrible and long-lasting depressions. She now hardly ever gets depressed, preferring instead to live a life of happiness. To change so radically does take much time and effort, but it can be done.

Rebirth in the Moment

With meditation it is possible to come to see that 'self' is not born just once in a lifetime. It does not come into being only with physical birth and then stay the same throughout life. No, self is actually born many times a day. Self is born, in a perfectly literal sense, every time the idea-of-myself arises.

Whenever we get affronted, annoyed, threatened or distressed it is due to the idea-of-self arising. Whenever we feel that we are missing something or that we are inadequate in some way it *always* arises on the idea-of-self. It always arises on the comparison of one 'separate self' with another 'separate self'. This is birth—and it happens not only with the painful things but also with the pleasant things. Whenever the idea-of-self arises, either in connection with distress or in connection with happiness, then that is the arising of Samsara. That is the arising of birth and the promise of death, for whatever is born must also die.

Whatever deliberate action we make, whether for the good or for the bad, it will have consequences which are unavoidable. These consequences may be pleasant or unpleasant but they will always be impermanent. It does not matter what we try to achieve. It does not matter how good we become or what level of existence we manage to get reborn in—either on a momentary basis or for the next lifetime—the attainments we reach are all transient. They do not and cannot last. There is no lasting happiness within Samsara, the round of birth and death. This is the very problem with the endless and perpetual wandering. This is the meaning of the first noble truth expounded by the Buddha. There is no peace anywhere. Truly, there is suffering wherever we look in the round of birth and death.

If that were the whole story, then life would be grim indeed, but the Buddha's other three noble truths define, in their turn, the origin of this truly painful state of affairs, the total escape from suffering and, therefore, from all birth and death and, finally, the way and method that will lead one to that most desirable freedom. The Buddha's teaching is complete in itself. Nothing is missing. It is all there for those who wish to make use of it.

Buddhism and Sex

Sexuality is a subject which troubles many people at different times and at different stages along the meditative path. It is something about which there are all kinds of misconceptions. It is not as complicated as some people make it out to be but, at the same time, misunderstanding it causes endless anxiety and grief, and great personal difficulties.

I want to try to define for you what is 'right' and what is 'wrong' sex using those terms as they are used in relation to the right and wrong eightfold paths of Buddhism. 'Right' means perfect so, in this context, it would describe the perfect approach to sexuality. 'Wrong' on the other hand is an approach to sexuality which is deleterious to the individual and which takes him or her into painful and unrewarding areas of experience.

Many people—both in the East and the West—are very confused about sexuality. Being confused, they tend to undertake sexual practices which *in terms of the meditative path* are very deleterious. Of course some sexual practices are deleterious under any circumstances but I intend to cover only some aspects of sexuality which touch on the meditative path itself. What people choose to do or not do is entirely their own affair but I think that it has to be pointed out that, whilst some kinds of sexual behaviour are no bar whatsoever to reaching the highest states of which a human being is capable, certain other kinds completely block meditative progress. Whatever else those practices might do is not in question. What follows carries no individual value judgements. It is simply to illustrate what happens if certain things are done.

Right and Wrong Sexuality
Right or normal sexuality is *never* criticised by the majority of people in any culture. It is always fully accepted. It is never a problem. No matter what the legal system may say or not say, there is a certain clearly defined norm for a particular culture. It is this that one can define broadly as 'right sexuality'. On the other hand, wrong or abnormal sexual behaviour is *always* criticised by the majority. It is never fully accepted and it is always under attack in one way or another. This is true no matter what may or may not be incorporated into the laws of the country.

Why should this be so? Why should there be this quite overwhelming acceptance of certain kinds of sex and equally overwhelming rejection of other kinds? What is at the back of it all? To reach an answer to these questions we have to take a fresh look at the whole subject.

Masculine and Feminine Principles
What do we really mean by the word 'sex'? We use the word often without giving any thought at all to the different shades of meaning it has. It carries implications far, far beyond the mere physical activity that most people think of whenever the word is used.

It is helpful to consider human experience as divided into four different areas: physical, emotional, intellectual and 'spiritual', where spirit represents the urge towards wisdom and compassion. Whilst this is not as accurate as traditional Buddhist analysis, it nevertheless will help greatly to expand our understanding of the subject and is slightly easier to deal with for most people.

The most accurate way to describe sex is as the union of masculine and feminine principles. This covers a much greater scope than just the physical union of man and woman. The physical side of sex is of course very important—the male and female aspects are so obvious in the physical form—but also the physical can be seen as illustrating the activity of the male versus the passivity of the female. The masculine *principle* is activity; the feminine *principle* is passivity.

On the mental or intellectual level the masculine principle equates with the analytical mind which is able to penetrate into the facts of any matter in question and break it up into little pieces for examination. This analytical function is in stark contrast to the feminine, intuitive side of intellect which synthesises different things into an overall picture: it puts things together to make a greater unity.

On the emotional side, the masculine principle leans towards justice, towards impersonality, towards a fair assessment in an unbiased manner of whatever comes before the mind. In contrast the feminine principle is very much more personal in operation and is concerned to nurture and make whole in a quite definitely biased way. In any family it is usually the feminine principle which writes letters and keeps in touch with people.

In the spiritual dimension the masculine principle culminates in wisdom, the feminine principle in compassion.

Right sexual behaviour permits easy access to progress along the meditative path. Wrong sexual behaviour prevents meditative development. Wrong sexual behaviour has this effect because it always ignores one and sometimes both of the principles of masculinity and femininity. Ignoring one entire principle, it also ignores vital aspects of body, intellect, emotion and spirituality—and the individual suffers greatly as a result.

Sex and Celibacy

If right sexual behaviour is no bar to meditative development, why is it that those following the spiritual path full-time—for example, monks and nuns—are invariably celibate?

Celibacy too is an aspect of right sexual behaviour. Monks and nuns who indulge in active sexual behaviour are generally frowned upon in all cultures of the world. Celibacy is the norm for the recluse. There are however two distinct faces of the celibate, one right and one wrong.

The wrong face of celibacy is seen everywhere in the world although more frequently in the West. It is a face which is wizened and dried out. It seems somehow bitter and, most strikingly, it is sexless—you are not sure whether you are looking at a man or a woman. The right face of celibacy is an open face. It is a full face which is happy and very definitely male or female. Why is this? What is the difference between these two?

In the first case sexuality has been rejected. It has been put aside, sometimes violently. It has been repressed and this leads to a certain 'drying up' of the character of the individual.

In the second case, sexuality has been accepted and integrated into the life-style even though the individual is celibate. Sex is not ignored and rejected; it is recognised and acknowledged. True celibacy leads to a balanced and very dynamic life-style and is extremely beneficial not only to the individual but also to those around him or her as well.

These two mark the extremes of the celibate life. Celibacy can be negative and escapist or it can be positive and life-embracing.

Sex and the Meditative Path

Living a family life is no bar to spiritual evolution, providing always that sufficient meditative work is done. A word always to bear in mind in this context is 'attachment': where there is attachment there is difficulty. Where attachment is absent, progress is swift.

Normal sex as defined so far is absolutely no bar to progress and this would include the kind of celibacy that accepts sexuality, that does not repress it. Celibacy without repression is extremely rewarding although possible only for those who are able to let go of their attachment to the physical expression of the sexual urge.

We can further define 'normal' sex as that which is not promiscuous in any way, certainly not adulterous, nor lecherous. It is the kind of sex that the majority could be said to approve of. I have heard it described as sex within marriage for all cultures but, if we say that, we have to bear in mind that definitions of marriage vary widely across the world and I think that a better definition would be sex within long-standing heterosexual relationships rather than marriage as such.

Abnormal sex on the other hand, wrong sex, is always a problem and always holds up meditative progress. Let us look at it more closely.

Wrong Sexual Behaviour
There are various kinds of wrong sexual behaviour, promiscuity being one of the most obvious. Over-indulgence of any kind is always based in craving or fear and has simple sensuality as its objective; the individual seeks sensuality and nothing else. Some people indulge in group sex for the same reasons: they wish to experience sensuality and physical union only. They often treat their partners as sex objects. There is little or no thought given to the mental union or the emotional union and the thought of spiritual union never crosses the mind. It is materialism pure and simple. It is to go on the wrong path through craving, through craving for sensuality. This means that the individual, in seeking his own advantage, is actually choosing a path which will *increase* his frustration and distress rather than ease it, as he hopes.

41

Another aspect of wrong sex is masturbation accompanied by deliberately constructed sexual fantasy. One of the problems with such behaviour is that there is no actual union of the masculine and feminine principles. There is a perversion of the completely natural desire for union by building a fantasy which is free from any kind of obligation to a human partner. In many cases fear of responsibility is the major cause of such behaviour and it marks someone who goes on the wrong path through fear or hatred. There may be fear of the personal restrictions of time and energy that accompany a relationship: a man might have to work to support financially more people than just himself; a woman might have radically to adapt her way of living to fit in with someone else. There may be a hatred of the very idea of 'getting involved' or even of the unquenchable life force which flows through every individual and which, under normal circumstances, drives him or her to seek a partner of the opposite sex.

Homosexuality is another problem area. Both male and female homosexuality imply a denial of one or another facet of the life stream, whether it is masculine or feminine. It is a curious thing that this rejection of the opposite polarity is often accompanied by an imitation of some of its other qualities: the male homosexual may adopt female mannerisms and the lesbian may sometimes look aggressively male. Such behaviour is a confusion of the desire to blend the masculine and feminine principles. It is to go on the wrong path through hatred and it holds up progress on the meditative path no matter how much the practice may be condoned by the laws of the country and no matter that it appears physically quite harmless in itself—although with the increase in AIDS one begins to wonder... The rejection of one polarity which always accompanies homosexuality is a major stumbling block to the integration and transcendence of masculinity and femininity which signifies real progress on the meditative path.

A slightly worse problem than homosexuality is celibacy with repression. It is quite common for lay people who belong to a religious group—including Buddhist ones—to feel that progress is only to be made by abjuring sex altogether, and to attempt the impossible by not having anything to do with any aspect of sexuality.

To attempt to deny sexuality altogether is to attempt to deny life itself. Such a rejection of both masculine and feminine polarities is usually based on a fear of the sexuality within the individual and any sexual urge is deliberately pushed down out of sight so it cannot interrupt the search for the ideal. It is a refusal to acknowledge reality and runs directly counter to the direction of the true spiritual aspirant. This is celibacy *with* repression where the suppression of sexuality has become so habitual that it has been lost from awareness.

People repressing sexuality in this way often seem too nice for their own good. They seem 'too good to be true' and it is tempting to see if it is possible to provoke them in some way so that they show what is really there, under the surface but hidden from view. Nearly everyone will have met such an individual. Such repression is to go on the wrong path through fear or hatred: fear of the responsibility involved in trying to blend the masculine and feminine elements; a fear too, perhaps, of being swept out of control by sexuality; a fear, maybe, of not making progress on the meditative path because sex rears its head.

Sex and Self-Expression

You can nearly always tell those who are devoted to abnormal sexual practices because their self-expression is in some way distorted. Not long ago I saw a nun walking along the road: her face was lined, bitter and twisted, and the mouth pinched as if she were sucking on a slice of lemon. She looked as though she were nursing a giant hatred for herself and for the world. 'How sad,' I thought. 'Such a person would be far better off out in the world, living life to the full and learning about things, learning about herself *that* way rather than trying to cut off the stream of life which flows through her.'

With any kind of distorted sexual practice the self-expression becomes twisted in some manner which is visible to those who know how to see. Such distortion means that those people cannot progress beyond a certain point on the meditative path. They will have to transform their sexual behaviour patterns first.

Why should abnormal sexual practices be such a hindrance? Why should they be such an obstacle? Wrong sexual behaviour always is based on a denial and rejection of the true union of masculine and feminine principles.

Integrating Masculinity and Femininity

To make progress towards enlightenment there has to be an understanding of both the masculine and the feminine; there has to be the melding of the masculine and the feminine. Normal sexuality celebrates this union as far as it can. The complete union—on the physical level, the emotional level, the mental level and the spiritual level—is possible only with the total acceptance of masculinity and femininity, both in oneself and externally. It doesn't matter where you start. You have to accept feminine and masculine principles externally and internally—in the world around you, which means in other people, and in yourself.

This means that men have to acknowledge and develop the softer side of their nature, the compassionate side. Women need to acknowledge and develop their analytical skills and their impartiality. These are not qualities which have to be *created*: they already exist even if they are not very active. For instance, women, far more than men, are survivors. They can be so realistic that it is quite frightening for the male who, for all his rational intellect, is often so in love with ideals that he cannot see straight. There has to be a coming together of these two poles, these two opposites, if the mind is to become truly balanced.

The popular image of men includes such qualities as aggression, power, dominance, mechanical skill, intellect or reason, courage, independence and strength of will. The popular image of women includes qualities such as love, compassion, nurturing, home-building, intuition, compromise, submission and emotionality. These popular images are like cartoon characters which represent different facets of the real state of affairs. We cannot take them too seriously. However, they do give us a guide to *what we think of* as masculinity and femininity and, to that extent, they are very useful. Most people try to regulate their behaviour by a set of ideas like these.

A man will try to appear courageous, for example, and may well feel less of a man if he is unable to. Similarly, many a man will violently oppose any suggestion that he has any of the 'feminine' qualities such as compassion or intuition, for it seems to undermine his maleness. In a similar way, a woman may worry about not being a good home-builder or about the fact that she seems sometimes to hate the children she is supposed always to love and nurture. She may also vehemently reject any suggestion that she has any mechanical skills to the extent of not being able to change a plug or clean out a drain.

The meditator is trying to uncover and eliminate personal prejudices of this kind. In doing so, his or her behaviour becomes more rounded and less role-dominated. The successful meditator is one who is able to express any of the 'masculine' and 'feminine' qualities without feeling in any way threatened.

If one can come to the acceptance of both principles and meld them together in the one being, then that acceptance leads to the ultimate flowering of love. Love is not chauvinistic, it is not partial; it is all-embracing. That all-embracing love has the same flavour as enlightenment itself for it has transcended the opposites, it has gone beyond simple masculine and feminine, it has gone beyond male and female, it has gone beyond man and woman. It has brought together and finally transcended all opposites. To make progress on the meditative path it is imperative to come to a clear understanding and acceptance of masculinity and femininity.

The Whole Person
One of the difficulties with the whole subject of sexuality is that you can stumble along for years without seeming to do any harm to yourself or others by the things you do. Ignoring one or the other polarity seems to work well enough if judged from the point of view of functioning in the day-to-day world and a lot of people get along for a lot of years without taking too much notice of these opposite poles. If an individual takes up the path of meditation, however, the situation changes dramatically. Meditators are forced into taking notice: that is the whole point of the meditative path. When they become aware of the opposite poles of masculinity and femininity within themselves they have some difficult and courageous decisions to make. Those courageous decisions may lead to acknowledging parts of themselves which they literally live in fear of but, as with all apparently risky ventures, there is a lot to be gained.

Acknowledging what one might see as the darker side of oneself brings with it tremendous benefits, a freeing up, a spontaneity, an outrush of feeling that is quite beautiful when it happens. You begin to understand just what is meant by the statement that enlightenment can be seen as wisdom and compassion. It has the wisdom to see all sides of the coin, see all sides of life, and the compassion not to blame anything or anyone, not to criticise anything or anyone, but to accept it all just as it is. In that way, however close you can get to it, the acceptance of the two opposing principles is the quickest way through the meditative path. With such acceptance you will have no more problems with sex and sexuality, with masculinity and femininity.

Sex and sexuality cover far, far more than just physical sex. The subject covers the whole gamut of active and passive principles on four quite distinct levels: physical, mental or intellectual, emotional and—for want of a better word—spiritual.

☆

Question: *Is open celibacy one of mindfulness of the arising of sexual desire?*
Answer: Yes, most definitely. That's a very great part of it. And recognising that when sexual desire arises, it is normal, natural and entirely to be welcomed as a symptom of a healthy body and mind. Also that it is completely inevitable if you are in a male/female intermix. And also to recognise that you don't *have* to do anything about it. Simply recognise it and it will pass away. It is a tremendously difficult area because people seem to think that if sexuality arises, this being the 'instant everything' culture, you should gratify it straight away. They think that if you *can't* do something about it immediately, then you have a problem, so the best thing to do, they think, is to smash down the sexuality in some way such as taking a cold shower or extreme physical exercise. Push it down, get rid of it, keep it out of sight. And that way you start doing damage, especially if that practice becomes established and therefore apparently effective, so that at the merest hint of sexuality there is a rigid, automatic and almost unconscious reaction which says NO.

That is what some monks and nuns get into. They get scared of the uprush of sexual feeling, even though it is perfectly normal, and they smash it down so hard that it never sees the light of day again through normal channels and starts to work its way out through all kinds of other less blocked channels and therefore comes out distorted. One thing is certain: you can never push it down and keep it down. It has got to come out somehow. It always has to. It is life itself.

Sex is not a problem except that you make it one. You make it a problem by feeling guilty about it when it is, after all, a normal physiological reaction or by *not* feeling guilty about it at all and going wild.

If through meditation one becomes aware of a mental characteristic of masculinity or femininity which is more dominant than the others in oneself, is there anything one can do to encourage the development of the opposite characteristic so as to become more balanced?

Yes there is, usually. A great deal depends on character so I'll have to generalise. Don't think that what follows necessarily applies to you. It may not. You have to approach this area of masculinity and femininity very carefully.

In general, women need to sharpen up the masculine side of the mind. Women therefore need to develop more drive and determination and not be so influenced by their emotions. For example, women will tend to give up the meditation session when 'not in the mood'. This is to form a judgement on a basis of feeling rather than on a basis of intellect. Men will tend always to do the meditation, no matter how they feel, reasoning in an intellectual manner that it is not possible to become accomplished at something unless it is worked at steadily. For women to balance the feminine aspect of emotionality, then, they need to ensure that they do the meditation practice whether in the mood or not. They need to learn to analyse things clearly, they need to learn to be impersonal and to be able to observe impersonally, and they need to learn how to be active on a meditative level, which means that they need to be able to direct the mind at the meditation object in a positive and persistent way *today* rather than saying, 'I'll just take it easy now but I'll really get down to working hard tomorrow.'

Men on the other hand suffer from the opposite problem of too much aggressiveness, determination, intellectuality and reliance on mere logic. Men need on an intellectual level to learn how to be passive and to encourage the synthetic function of the mind, the aspect which gathers things together and presents an answer. On the emotional level, men need to be softer, they need to be more nurturing, more compassionate, they need to be tolerant of their own and other people's faults. In terms of the spiritual search, men continually direct and control the meditation, putting in vast quantities of energy in the intellectual belief that the secrets of reality must reveal themselves before sufficient relentless pressure. They need to learn how to be passive and inactive and simply to observe sounds, feelings, thinking and hearing come and go, rather than putting a lot of energy into 'making progress'.

Once you begin to see how these two polarities can blend together, you begin to see that it is possible to find a harmonious balance without doing damage to either polarity, and that is the important thing. It is not a 'seek and destroy' mission at all. It is a 'love and nurture' mission.

You need to identify each aspect of masculinity and femininity which is strong for you and firstly and most importantly accept it as it is. You do not have to act on it but you do have to accept it. Accepting it you are already halfway out of the wood. At that stage it may well help to take upon yourself the discipline of trying deliberately to encourage the opposite polarity that corresponds to the function you are concerned with. For instance, if you find that you tend to be a very aggressive person, with that masculine quality well in evidence, it would be beneficial to take up the practice of loving kindness meditation to develop the complementary feminine quality of patience or tolerance. If, on the other hand, you find yourself so ready to place your faith in things that appear good and wholesome that you sometimes lack intellectual discrimination, which is a feminine tendency, then take up the intellectual study of spiritual works to refine the mental discrimination. In that way you have the strength of aggression tempered with love or the beauty of faith balanced by intelligent assessment. You have both rather than neither.

The Family

Everyone is someone's child and many of you are mothers and fathers as well. All of you therefore have considerable experience of family relationships but whether you understand them and can handle them emotionally may be another matter. Tonight I want to introduce you to what Buddhism has to say on this both complicated yet most sensitive of topics, as well as what changes in attitude towards your family you can expect to find as a result of meditating. For the purposes of tonight's talk I am limiting family to parents and children rather than the extended network of family relationships which some people enjoy.

Childhood Conditioning

The best place to start the subject of the family is right at the beginning, with the child. From birth we are conditioned by the views fed to us by others, including mother, father, grandparents, teachers, priests, neighbours, television and radio. All of these people and these communication media have views about the way life is and the way life should be and these views are fed to us through their words and actions. We absorb attitudes to life from the very atmosphere, so to speak; we take them in unconsciously and then, at a later date, we give them out to others as if they were our own, usually not realising that they are second-hand.

Attitudes and views which we absorb in this way, although unconscious, strongly influence the way in which we think and act. Sometimes these views and attitudes to life are efficient and guide us well in our day-to-day living. On other occasions they are dangerously inefficient for our character-type, even though they may be right for our parents. If we don't realise that we are acting on one of these inefficient, conditioned views then we suffer great mental torment as we act against our own best interests. We end up being really puzzled about life and very confused about our own part in it.

The Western View of the Child

Western conditioning is to regard the new-born baby as innocent, as fresh, as having no loves or hates or 'hang-ups': it is believed to be a 'blank slate'. This view is inevitable if there is no concept of rebirth in the society, and the average Westerner firmly believes that we do not exist before birth and that when we die, *that is it*; it's the end, finished, *kaput*, all is over; there is nothing after death but a big black void. In Buddhism, this is known as the annihilationist view.

Conditioned by the annihilationist view, our attitude to a new-born child is that it is *only* a physical shell; it is mentally and emotionally empty and unformed. It's born a nothing, innocent of all knowledge, so it must be moulded and shaped; it must be 'created' by its parents and must be taught how to walk, talk, eat, feel and think. Thus if some great disaster befalls the child when it's very young—perhaps it gets run over by a car or contracts an incurable disease or gets kidnapped and sexually assaulted—then the parents are heartbroken, devastated, bitter and resentful that such a thing should happen to their innocent baby.

As far as the parents are concerned their baby has committed no wrong. In their eyes, it's too young to have done *anything* to deserve such suffering so why should this terrible disaster befall it? 'After all it's only a child', is the cry you hear. That cry may just as well be, 'It's only an empty, shapeless vessel. What could an empty container possibly have done wrong? It is totally unfair and unjust that it should experience such harm and pain.'

Is it, though? Is the young child an empty, shapeless thing, free from all blame and guilt? Is it 'innocent' in the way Western parents think?

The Buddhist View of Birth

Where does the child's relationship with the family actually start? Is it when the child can talk, or before that? Buddhism would suggest that the child's relationship with its family starts long before its own birth; it starts with intercourse. The individual-to-be-born is attracted by the act of sexual intercourse, finding one or other of the partners particularly attractive and craving to be part of the action. This craving is significant because, in order for conception to take place at all, three things have to come together at the same time: a woman who is fertile, a man who is fertile and the being-to-be-born. If any of these three factors is missing then no conception can take place. If they are all present then, barring complications, nine months later a child is born to a proud mother and father.

The child has chosen to be born into that particular family and not into another one. It has chosen, consciously or unconsciously, by its former physical, verbal and mental actions. Past actions have brought about various results, among them being a need for a particular kind of family and environment. The being fits into a certain family rather like a piece into a jigsaw puzzle: many pieces in a jigsaw puzzle superficially look alike but in fact there is only one appropriate place for each piece.

In past lives we chose to think, to speak and to act physically in certain ways, thus 'choosing' our future place of birth by the inevitable outcome of those past actions. The choosing of a particular family is not often conscious, but it is a choice rather than something which is randomly determined. It is a resultant or outcome of kamma, deliberately chosen volition or action. Such volitions have results which affect our time, place and conditions of birth.

The Buddhist view is that that child is not an empty nothing at birth but is in fact an adult locked up in a child's body. It is a being that has lived hundreds and hundreds of lifetimes before as an adult and comes into this world complete with a fully developed set of cravings, hatreds, resentments, loves and joys. From the moment it is born it will attract to itself specific people and events drawn by its present mental qualities which result from its efficient and inefficient habitual actions performed in the past. What's more, before it is born it chooses the environment and the family which is best suited to attract the necessary disasters and successes towards it. This way it can learn lessons, evolve and grow on its journey towards becoming a fully integrated individual.

A being knows before it is born both the high and the low points of its future human life; it chooses them. For example, an individual may choose a life where, as a child, he will be run over by a 'hit-and-run' driver, be left to die in the road, but will survive and take years to recover. That experience could be chosen for any number of reasons. It may be because he hit and knocked down a child in a previous life and callously felt no compassion or remorse. Now he needs to reduce callousness and develop a greater sympathy with others—which can be done by experiencing the lot of the victim. Another reason could be that the being is spiritually evolved and wishes to develop deep and subtle understanding by learning to cope properly with one very painful and drastic event, or it could be that he loves dearly the beings who are to be his new parents; he owes them something, and wishes to help *them* to grow spiritually by providing an event which will drive them to question many of their assumptions about birth, death, suffering and the purpose of life on earth.

It is a sad but true fact that most of our inner, spiritual

growth comes through painful events: at such times we desperately 'soul-search'; we turn inwards seeking answers to questions in an attempt to understand our suffering.

There is a host of possible reasons why an individual would regard being severely injured at the age of three as an unavoidable and necessary growth experience but, whatever the reason, the parents of the child will suffer dreadfully if they have no understanding of rebirth, no understanding of actions and their results, no understanding of the purpose of life and no understanding of the part the family unit plays in that purpose.

Perhaps you have never given any thought to the possibility that the family has a purpose other than raising children. In the overall scheme of things, the family unit is a rarity, which points to the fact that there is far more to it than is at first obvious.

The Family and Other Planes of Existence

Buddhism distinguishes a total of thirty realms of existence in addition to the human one. Some of them, the deva and brahma realms, are more pleasant than the human, others are more unpleasant and include the animal realm and the demon and hell realms.

In twenty-nine of these thirty-one realms there is no such thing as the family unit as we know it. It is unknown for a man and a woman to come together, produce a child, and then for the three of them to live together for fifteen to twenty years until the child is strong enough and skilled enough in the ways of the world to leave the family nest. The only other realm that has a family unit is the animal kingdom and there the parents and offspring stay together for a comparatively short time.

In all the other twenty-nine planes of existence, birth takes place spontaneously; one just appears there, totally developed and with all one's faculties fully grown. On these planes there is no need to go through the awkward baby stage and be protected and looked after by adults.

As it is only the human realm which has a family structure lasting for a relatively long time, it seems reasonable to wonder if there isn't somewhat more to the family unit than simple, physical protection for the growing child. As a further consideration, it is only in the human realm that conditions are balanced enough in terms of pleasure and pain for a being to become enlightened, should he or she make a conscious effort in that direction.

The Hidden Purpose of the Family
The deeper purpose of the mother/child, father/child, husband/wife, brother/sister relationships is to provide conditions which aid us in our evolution towards enlightenment.

Family relationships last for a long time; about twenty years of daily contact between parents and child and perhaps from ten to fifty years of daily contact between husband and wife. In a long-term relationship you have constantly in front of you the example of another person's character. You have many and various clues as to how to develop a certain character trait that you may be lacking, as well as how to prevent an undesirable trait from getting worse. For example, if you find you react violently against a particular quality in a certain family member the chances are that you actually have that quality yourself, even though you may not be conscious of it. Perhaps you over-developed it in the past, in a past life even, so now you turn against that quality, which ensures that you do not attempt to develop it any further. Seeing that particular mental quality in a sister or father shows you what an obnoxious trait it is, and makes you resolve not to be like that.

Another example, but this time of how constant contact helps to develop a quality we might lack. Quite a common husband/wife combination is that of the forceful, dogmatic, super-confident male and the shy, timid, gentle and unconfident woman. The woman, desperately lacking confidence, feels a sense of non-fulfilment and unbalance, and selects a mate who has enough confidence and aggression for two. This makes her feel whole. He, on the other hand, lacks the soft, gentle touch and looks for a partner who has these qualities, thereby making him feel relaxed and cared-for when they are together. What each needs to learn is how personally to develop the quality that the partner displays, thereby to become more skilled as a human being.

The female needs to learn to be more confident and she has a very good teacher in her husband. Being exposed daily to his super-confidence she cannot help but absorb the mental and physical characteristics that go to make up the 'confident personality'. If she should refuse to put into practice the lessons she is being taught, she will have a love/hate relationship with her husband. She will feel magnetically attracted to him because he has this quality that she subconsciously wishes to develop in herself and yet she will often find herself repulsed by what she calls his vulgar, super-salesman confidence.

The husband needs to learn to balance his aggression with gentleness and softness. He must learn to be less confident of his own opinions occasionally, and not always assume he's right about everything. He has before him a perfect example in the personality of his wife. They are one another's teachers.

The World Myth

There is a myth believed in by all peoples of the world, regardless of race, nationality or where on the globe they dwell. It is the myth which says that a family must always be happy, united, intimate, loving and supporting. It is the myth that parents must be wise, infinitely tolerant and must give out unconditional love, always.

How many families do you know which fit that description? Most families have fights; they squabble; they cry; they resent one another; they communicate only occasionally. Of course, *sometimes* they seem to come close to the ideal and there is lots of love around, and laughter and fun and fierce loyalty. Parents are wise in patches, tolerant when they are in the mood and can only manage love on a conditional basis. They say, with actions if not words, 'I'll love you when you're good but will withdraw that love when you're bad. I'll love you when you do well at school but will withdraw that love if you get bad grades.' Parents can't manage anything other than conditional love because that is what they apply to themselves. A human being cannot love another totally unless he loves himself totally and he can only do that when he has eradicated craving and hatred. It is only the enlightened man or woman who is capable of unconditional, therefore total, love.

We get worried, frustrated and miserable when we are ensnared by belief in the world myth of the always-harmonious, always-loving family. As soon as a mother gets angry with her child and rows with it, she suffers agonies of guilt and self-recrimination. Why? Because she compares her behaviour with that of the 'super-mum' of the world myth, and knows that she has failed (again!) to achieve it all the time. She does not see that the ideal is factually impossible to achieve, because the super-mum is not human. No human super-mum could ever exist. No family unit past, present or future has ever managed or will ever manage to be harmonious and loving all day and every day.

When a mother compares her own short temper and irritability with the mental image she holds of the ever-patient, loving super-mum, she finds that the two images do not match. Arising dependent upon that comparison come feelings of self-hatred, doubt and lack of confidence in her capacity to be a good mother. If she didn't have the super-image as a comparison, she would have only her own current experience to deal with and then there would be no problem. She causes herself distress through the comparison with something that cannot possibly exist. Comparisons really are the root cause of all suffering. They could be called the major evil in the world.

Clinging to the world myth, we keep comparing our actual family life with what we think family life *should* be and find we are unable to abandon our distress. The purpose of meditation is to become aware of the existence of comparisons and to see how to put a stop to comparison for good. As we begin to abandon comparisons, the light gradually dawns. We begin to see that the real family bears little relation to the myth and that there is a very good reason for it being as it is. The purpose of the family is *not* to make us happy. Happiness is a by-product, it is not the main aim of relationships, family or otherwise. The purpose of the family unit is to assist us to develop and to evolve. For certain character-types an unhappy family life is essential to their evolution.

When you see this, and abandon belief in the world myth, then whatever family you were born into or have created yourself through marriage will be seen as absolutely perfect. The family unit you live in now is perfect for you and for all its members. The family unit you lived in in the past was exactly what all its members needed at the time.

Reasons for Choosing a Family
Making a conscious and deliberate choice of family is possible only for those beings who are either so good at concentration meditation or so evolved that they can actually select consciously the exact conditions of the future birth.

Some years ago I knew a boy who had been a Buddhist monk in a previous life. He had had certain psychic capacities well developed in that life and had wished to be born in close proximity to a friend whom he had been close to through many lifetimes. At the time of his last death, when he was a monk, the nearest he could get to his companion of many lifetimes was to be born into a family that associated with his friend, who had no immediate family himself. That monk consciously and deliberately *chose* to be born near to his old companion. His prime interest was in his friend rather than the environment or the family he chose to be born in.

Most individuals will not be conscious of the choice they make although that choice will be based upon similar considerations to the example just quoted. A being will choose to be born into a certain family either because it has strong emotional and karmic links with one or both of the parents, or because it needs to experience the society in which the parents live, or because the being needs to be close to someone in that family's neighbourhood, as in the story I've just narrated.

When the connection is with the parents it means that either they were parents, children, brothers, sisters or friends in a previous life, or that they were enemies. You can imagine the underlying tension that will exist in a family where a parent and child are former enemies.

Sometimes a child will choose to be born into a certain family not because it has previous connections with any member of that family but because the attitudes towards life of the parents and other family members serve as a counterbalance to its own personality.

There is an example of this in the Edgar Cayce files. A 'life reading' was taken for a five-year-old child. The child was noted to be selfish, unwilling to admit when he was wrong, and indifferent. His outlook was likened to that of a research scientist because he was so impersonal and was dedicated purely to intellectual values. The reading showed that in his previous life he had devoted himself to steam as an instrument of power. Before that he had worked with chemical explosives and before that he had been absorbed in mechanics. During a life in Atlantis he had been an electrical engineer. Four past lifetimes dedicated to pure science had produced a being wholly concerned with intellect, theory, speculation and analysis at the expense of love, beauty, friendship and feeling.

It would have been reasonable to expect the child to have chosen to be born into a family with a scientific background but instead he chose to be born into a family that was very idealistic and impractical. The value-system of the father was distinctly social and religious and the mother, like the father, took part in social service activities. The elder brother was an idealist whose main concern in life was helping other people.

Thus the child as he grew up was always confronted with a value system different from his own. This helped him to correct an unhealthy over-balance which had gone too far towards the dry sciences.

Personal Growth and Evolution
Most would label as a bad environment one where the housing is poor, the food scarce, the schooling inadequate and the neighbourhood undesirable and disturbed by frequent occurrences of murder, rape and mugging. Similarly, a 'bad' family would be seen as one in which the father is a drunkard or the mother a prostitute or where the child is subjected to heavy beatings. All of these conditions are considered by most people as undesirable, unfortunate and not conducive to the proper development of a child.

Bearing in mind that a being chooses to be born into a family or environment which helps to meet its needs, then there can be no such thing as either a 'bad' family or a 'bad' environment. If an entity chooses to be born into a specific environment, then that environment contains just what the being needs and it is not in fact deleterious *for that individual*. It is the right one for it, for it is only within that 'bad' environment that there are the right pressures and opportunities for it to evolve on its journey towards enlightenment.

If a child's mother beats it frequently and it finds the beatings unpleasant, it is nevertheless still right for it. Inefficient action that the child has performed previously has attracted violence towards it in the form of a mother with a bad temper. If the child can learn how to handle its response to that violence then some healthy internal growth can occur.

Some beings develop artistic talents, or educational talents, or efficient personality traits, only if they are 'up against it'. Under more favourable conditions they may be just too lazy to bother.

It is shortsighted to assume that efficient personal growth can take place only in peaceful and plentiful surroundings. Each human being is unique and the family and environment which suits one can most definitely be unsuitable for another.

Parental Attitudes and Meditation
If the parents' inner knowledge is not strong enough then the difficulties their children experience may become an almost intolerable burden to them. If they do not know that a child chooses to be born into a certain environment and chooses the subsequent events and people that come into its life, then the parents will suffer deeply when the child meets a problem, whether that problem be one of an incurable disease at the age of eight, or an unhappy marriage at the age of twenty-eight.

They will make no allowance for the fact that the child has its own qualities of character which are just as strong and as fully developed as their own and with which the child will resist or adapt to its environment to meet its own particular needs. The wrong view that the child is the sole creation of the parents is the source of much child/parent conflict. It breeds in the parents possessiveness and a strong craving for the child to behave in a way calculated to fulfil their dreams. Any sign of deviation from the course they have planned causes the parents tremendous anxiety and stress.

With this wrong view, parents will tend to blame themselves if a child grows up badly, jumping to the conclusion that they didn't provide enough education for their child, or that they argued too much in front of it, or that they didn't have enough money to provide the good things in life. They tell themselves fairy stories and say *if only* they had been able to provide one or all of these things then perhaps their child would have turned out better.

With meditation and much thought given to the teachings of the Buddha all such wrong views begin to crumble, gradually wearing away until they are replaced by an accurate picture of the true state of affairs. With the development of this right understanding, recriminations and self-blame are cut out. Parents know that the child is an individual in its own right and that they are only the supporting conditions to help that being achieve its self-chosen life tasks. This attitude enables them to maintain much more balance and equanimity when the child meets with an accident or a problem. They understand that they have done the best they can for the child, given their own conditions and capabilities.

Any difficulties the child experiences in responding to the conditions provided by the parents are its own responsibility. The child chooses to respond either efficiently or inefficiently according to its own mental habit patterns.

Personal Responsibility
A child is a being with full responsibility for its own responses. A story of two brothers, first told by a New York psychiatrist, illustrates this rather well.

There were two brothers, both six years old. They were identical twins; so identical that they even had the same freckle in the same spot. In spite of being so similar physically nobody ever had any trouble telling them apart because one was a cheerful little optimist; whenever you looked at him he always smiled. The other was a pessimist; he was always gloomy and sulky.

Their mother took them to a psychiatrist and said, 'Doctor, I don't want much, just balance them off a bit—one a little bit more, the other a little bit less.'

The doctor said, 'OK, this is what you have to do. When their next birthday rolls around give the pessimist plenty of toys. More toys than he's ever had in his life before.'

'What do I do for the optimist?' the mother asked.

'For the optimist you buy a bag of manure. These different presents will balance them off a bit.'

On their next birthday, she did just what the doctor suggested and gave the twins their presents.

After a while she opened the bedroom door to see what was happening and there, sitting in the middle of the floor surrounded by masses of the most beautiful toys, was the little pessimist. His sole comment was, 'Look at this bunch of junk. I don't like these toys. The boy next door has *better* toys.'

She then looked at the optimist. He had his head buried in the bag and was digging furiously through the manure saying, 'You can't fool me. Where there's a pile of manure there must be a pony.'

Everyone experiences pleasant and unpleasant sensory objects and life events. It is your own attitude towards those objects which determines whether you suffer or not.

Meditation and Personal Responsibility

The purpose of meditation is to become aware of the existence of comparisons, to see how you suffer each time you do compare, and to learn how to put a stop to comparison for good.

From vipassana meditation practice we come to learn how inefficient it is to compare. We discover that we make a comparison when we want our husband or wife or mother or father or child to behave differently. Wanting them to be different causes us a lot of pain and, through the meditation, we come to see that the way to decrease this suffering is to stop comparing our family members with what we want them to become. Letting go of the comparison, we become more settled and more at peace with ourselves and our family.

We also learn from the meditation that the more we become conscious of ourselves and understand how our minds work the more we are capable of understanding the other members of the family. This improves our communication with them. We realise why they are as they are and that they cannot be any other way, given their personalities and the relationship between those particular personalities and the environment. This makes us more tolerant, more understanding and more patient.

Meditating, in the correct manner and consistently, reduces our cravings and hatreds. When these are reduced we have more time available to listen to the problems of our children or marriage partner or parents. When we are angry or depressed, or when we desire things to be other than they are, then we demand that those around us listen to *us* and pay attention to *us*. With these inefficient states obsessing the mind we demand a lot of time and energy from others. We take rather than give.

Meditation does much to change for the better our attitudes to our families. Changed personal attitudes ensure that we experience maximum internal growth and that growth is accompanied by a reduction in stress in our family relationships, which makes life very much more pleasant and very much more rewarding.

Inner Wealth

The main reason for meditating is to become conscious of those areas of mind which are unconscious. It is these unconscious aspects which drive us to do, say and think in certain set patterns. Some of these patterns are healthy and therefore bring happiness in their wake. Others are unhealthy, causing us distress.

Without the decision to make these unconscious facets of mind conscious they just ramble on, *ad infinitum*, running down the same old grooves that they have worn over many lifetimes, making us do, say and think things we'd rather not.

Usually, the only part of the process of which we are conscious is the end result; that sometimes we are sad, depressed or irritable and sometimes we are happy, excited or tranquil. Why these states pop into mind, we have no idea.

For the vast majority of the world's population, becoming conscious of unconscious areas of mind is of little interest. People don't see the profit in it. They only see that more is to be gained by obtaining wealth in the form of educational, artistic or sporting talents or in the form of property, TVs, cars, children, social position and the like. Increasing one's talents or increasing one's material goods is to add to oneself. This 'adding', this acquisition, is the way in which external wealth is built up.

After one talent or material possession has been acquired then one's sights are set on the next possession. Each possession added to oneself is seen as increasing one's happiness. If it just so happens that one doesn't get happiness from the acquisition of the last possession one had set one's heart on, well, never mind, happiness is promised just over the horizon with the next new possession: the new dish-washer, the new promotion at work, the new house or the new evening class. Adding things to oneself, as being the only way to happiness, is a firm belief that runs at a very deep level throughout all societies.

The Emptiness in the World
A few people in the world become conscious of the fact that no matter how many university degrees they get, how many pictures they paint or how many cars they acquire, somehow 'total, all-consuming happiness' still eludes them, and they're left with a nagging sense of emptiness. Some dismiss this inner nagging and cover it up with indulgence in drink or drugs, by going to parties or by espousing political causes.

Some do not ignore it. They decide that there must be a way of finding out what this nagging emptiness is. These few will then undertake a psychological or spiritual discipline to make conscious that nagging emptiness.

These few have begun their journey from unconsciousness to consciousness, from sleep to awakeness. These few have begun their journey towards inner wealth. Talents and goods are outer wealth which these few already have, even if, by most people's standards, they are as poor as church mice. They are externally wealthy because they have come to see the limitations of outer wealth and are content with however many or however few material possessions they have. However, as they outgrow the need to focus all their attention on outer wealth, they now find themselves perched on the edge of a vast, empty space.

That emptiness exists because they have no inner wealth. Their inner store-cupboard is bare. It has no goods in it. If externally they are wealthy but internally they are poor, this sets up an imbalance which they now become acutely aware of and set about to rectify.

The Laws of Inner Wealth
The laws that govern the acquisition of inner wealth are quite quite different from those that govern the acquisition of external wealth. We are raised from childhood to adulthood absorbing the rules that govern the acquisition of external wealth, but how to obtain inner wealth? That sort of conditioning just isn't there and so we go through quite a stressful time at the beginning of our inner training because we approach it in the same way as we do when acquiring outer wealth.

Our very first task is to learn to leave behind the laws governing the outer world and not to drag them through into this new universe we are trying to learn about. Once we have mastered that, then we can begin learning the rules that govern the acquisition of inner wealth. *This* wealth takes the form of becoming conscious of mind and the way in which mind operates.

In order to become conscious of mind one has to let go. One has to let go of thinking, let go of ill-will, let go of calm, let go of sleepiness, let go of tension. *Letting go* is the main law governing inner wealth. It is quite opposite to the law governing outer wealth. The law governing outer wealth is that of acquiring and hanging on. It's no wonder that we struggle when we come to build inner wealth. We want to continue that pattern of acquiring. For example, instead of simply letting go of ill-will, we attempt to overlay it by *adding* love to the mind. This is not true love. True love is that state which is present when we *let go* of everything, not when we try to add something to the mind. Let me give you an example.

69

Some time ago a student of ours who has been meditating for many years and who is very skilled at vipassana meditation was on a meditation retreat with us. In those days the road outside the House of Inner Tranquillity was plagued by motorbike enthusiasts so, at frequent intervals throughout the day, there would be this sudden shrill piercing sound of a motorbike engine as it tore with great speed either up or down the hill.

On one of these occasions he noticed running through his mind a series of pictures. He saw mental pictures of himself opening a window overlooking the road. Having opened the window he then saw himself get up on the window-sill and crouch there with machine gun in hand—and proceed to gun down every motorbike as it went past. That was followed by a further series of pictures with the same theme—getting rid of the noisy motorbikes—but in these images instead of using a machine gun he was laying huge tacks on the road to spike the motorbikes' tyres as they ran over them. These pictures popped into his mind, lasted for a while and then were gone. He recognised that such pictures were typical of his character; that such images ran through his mind from time to time; and he laughed.

It was his response to those pictures that was interesting. He was not disturbed by them. He didn't start hating himself for having such violent images. He didn't say to himself, 'I shouldn't be like this' and start criticising and tearing himself apart, and he didn't play around with the images and get passionately worked up with an enjoyment of them. He placed no value judgement of good or bad upon those images. To him they were just a series of objects that rose and fell in his mind and because he did not respond with either hate or lust towards them, they were like empty shells that just paraded past the mind's eye. The images had no real substance—even though they were perfectly clear—and he did not take them seriously at all. Because that meditator did not rise up with either lust or hate at the sight of those images, his mind remained undisturbed. It remained still. It remained peaceful. It remained harmless, even though the objects passing through would be given the label 'violent'.

It is one's *response* to internal objects which is critical. If there is a wanting for them to remain or a desire to get rid of them then there is attachment. When there is attachment, there is a refusal to let an object go. This refusal to let it go and pass out of existence causes a great laceration, a great pain in the mind. It is what is known as dukkha, suffering.

How to Meditate

We teach two basic meditations: the practice of insight, which leads to the complete eradication of suffering, and the practice of loving kindness, which smooths one's path through the difficulties of the world.

Instructions for the practice of insight meditation are quite straightforward, although putting those instructions into effect is always a little more difficult.

Insight meditation is practised in the following way. Decide for how long you are going to sit (half an hour would be best) and set a timer or alarm for the end of the period. Sit comfortably in an upright chair (there is no need whatsoever to sit on the ground cross-legged). Sit with the body erect, but not strained, and the eyes closed. Focus the attention on the feeling in the abdominal region, just above the navel. You will notice that the feeling seems to rise and fall as you breathe. Try to follow each 'rise' and each 'fall' of the feeling without letting your mind wander off to other things. This is the basis.

The first thing you discover is that you cannot do it for very long at all: the mind wanders off so very easily. To assist your concentration you can count, placing the number after each 'fall'. Count from 1 to 10 and then from 1 to 10 again, and again. You will find that two things may happen. Either the mind simply wanders off to something else and you forget the meditation and the counting, or you suddenly realise that you have got up to 14 or 15 or more. In both cases attention to the rise and fall has completely disappeared. You need to start watching and counting from the beginning again.

Doing just this watching and counting, repeatedly, you can become very concentrated and calm. You want to develop insight, however, and that means that you want to know what is going on a little more clearly than the practice as described will allow. To enhance attentiveness, you need to identify what is going on. Each time the mind wanders, make a mental note of what it was distracted by. If it was distracted by a worrisome thought, label it 'worry' and return to the rise and fall once again. If a sound pulls your attention away, say 'hearing'. If you find a pain to be the culprit, say 'painful feeling', and so on. Do not try to solve the problem you may be experiencing. Rather try simply to identify the type of distraction: it is the most effective way of labelling for this purpose.

Noticing what is going on is helped markedly if you refuse to give in to the temptation to move and wriggle about whilst sitting in meditation for the half-hour. Keep the eyes closed until the alarm sounds. Don't move. Keep noticing and when the mind wanders (as it will do most of the time to start with), simply label what it was distracted by and return to observing carefully the rise and fall. Do not alter the rate or depth of breathing to make the feeling stronger. Just sit. Just sit and watch and label.

Meditation and Inner Wealth

The whole purpose of placing the mind on rise and fall, time and time again, is to develop a skill: the skill of being conscious of an object in the moment. When you place the mind on rise and fall not only are you developing the ability to be conscious in the moment, but also you are developing the ability to narrow the focus of the mind on to one object. The former is known as mindfulness, the latter as concentration. These together form the skill of being conscious of an object in the moment. The skills of concentration and being-awake-in-the-present are being developed on a neutral object. We can't get too worked up about the rise and fall of the abdomen: we're not passionately in love with it, nor do we passionately hate it. We don't have any feeling towards it. It is neutral and as it is neutral, it is a particularly suitable object to use for developing the skills of concentration and mindfulness.

Having developed the ability to be conscious of an object in the moment we can't help but find the skill operating towards objects of which we would normally choose to be unconscious; objects such as jealousy, envy or loneliness. Normally we relegate these unpleasant objects down to the level of unconsciousness. We do this just by ignoring them; by pretending that we don't experience jealousy, for instance—we'll say, 'I'm not the jealous type.' However, when the skill of 'being conscious' is trained in, we find that we are incapable of ignoring these unpleasant objects—jealousy and all the rest—any longer.

Just being aware of them is not sufficient to take the sting out of them; they are still dangerous. To become aware of them is the first step in the process of acquiring inner wealth but that step must be followed by another. The second step in the process of acquiring inner wealth is to come to see what causes the arising and ceasing of objects.

The Dangers of Identification
For example, let's imagine you've gone to a public gathering of some kind—the Psychics and Mystics Fair, perhaps. There are all sorts of stalls at this fair, some dealing with health, some with diet and exercise. Other stalls deal with hypnotherapy, homoeopathy, acupuncture, tarot, yoga, astrology and meditation. Apart from the stalls there are also restaurants where you can purchase a tasty snack and a hall where lectures are held every hour. You attend one of these, on meditation, and after the lecture you strike up a conversation with the person sitting next to you. He, like you, meditates but belongs to a different group. He's heard, via the grapevine, of the group you belong to and has some

rather strongly antagonistic views to express on the type of meditation you're practising and the style of instruction your teacher uses. You get very upset.

You have been mindful of the conversation and, what's more, you've been mindful of your *reaction* to the conversation: you've watched the anger arise. However, it is not enough; just being aware that anger and indignation are present is not good enough. You need to be aware of *what the anger arose upon.* If you say that it arose because the person you were in conversation with said some unpleasant things about the meditation you practise, then you would be wrong. Sure he said some unkind things but they were only words, and words are only objects accompanied by, in this case, an unpleasant feeling. An object accompanied by an unpleasant feeling is not anger. So why did you choose to respond to his words with anger? Anger is suffering. Why did you choose to suffer?

Anger arose upon identification. You viewed what was being said in terms of 'my' meditation system, 'my' group, 'my' teacher. If the person had said something nasty about a system of meditation that you don't practise, or had said something nasty about the teacher in the next village, it wouldn't have bothered you. You probably would have laughed and enjoyed the 'put-down' of the other teacher. But dependent upon identification arises anger. That is, anger arises dependent upon viewing the group, the meditation system, the teacher as 'mine'.

The anger does *not* arise dependent upon unpleasant words being spoken by someone else. Anger arises upon a craving to get rid of the unpleasant feeling that accompanied those unpleasant words. The unpleasant feeling arose because of regarding the meditation system and teacher as 'mine'. When there is no clear seeing one doesn't notice that there is a craving to get rid of an unpleasant feeling. The actual details of the process pass by unnoticed and the wrong connection is made: the conclusion is drawn that it is Mr Smith's unpleasant words which are causing me pain, therefore it is Mr Smith's fault that I suffer. The truth of the matter is that it is not Mr Smith who caused me to suffer: I have caused myself to suffer.

That craving to get rid of the unpleasant feeling breeds a resistance to the words being spoken. If something disparaging is said about some other group then there is no identification and therefore no resistance. If I identify and regard it as 'my' group, 'my' meditation, 'my' teacher then there is resistance to the flow of reality and suffering arises.

It is important to see, to be mindful of, what suffering arises upon. If you are more than just mindful of the presence of ill-will, or envy, or jealousy; if you are also mindful of what ill-will, envy, or jealousy arise upon, then have you a chance of letting go of ill-will, envy, jealousy and all the rest that cause suffering. Only once you let go do you find you have inner wealth. As long as there is a hanging on to hatred, to bitterness, and to how the world *should* behave, then one's inner universe is empty. It's hollow. It's only filled with richness when objects are allowed to pass through, unhindered. Hanging on to any one of those fleeting objects brings about instant inner poverty. Letting go, even for an moment, starts the development of inner wealth.

Value Judgements and Inner Wealth

If you flick your right index-finger against your left wrist there arises a stinging sensation. Try it right now. That sensation is painful but you do not suffer even though you are experiencing an unpleasant object. Why is this? If a memory of a row with your wife or husband or parent or child comes into the mind you suffer. Both the stinging sensation and the memory of the row are unpleasant objects. The stinging sensation is painful but no suffering follows in its wake. The memory of the argument is also painful but, in this case, you suffer. Why should that be?

In this case you suffer because you put a value judgement on the disagreement and because you do not wish to experience the unpleasant feeling that the memory of the row arouses. That unpleasant feeling is pain but there is in fact no problem with pain as such. It is when you do not want to experience the pain that, instantly, you have a problem. The mind compares between what you are experiencing in the moment (pain) and what you would prefer to experience in the moment (non-pain). The instant the mind compares, there is suffering.

Whenever you base an action on a value judgement you open the door to suffering. If you judge an action to be personally damaging then you experience a painful memory/feeling as a result. If you judge an action to be personally favourable, then you experience a pleasant memory/feeling as a result—but suffer when the memory/feeling fades away and disappears.

With the stinging sensation there is no value judgement. You do not mind the stinging, even though, according to the rules of what constitutes an unpleasant object, you must call it painful and unpleasant. Because you do not mind the unpleasant, stinging sensation you do not compare it with what you would prefer to experience. Because you do not compare, you do not hang on to the pain; you let go of it. When you let go of an object, you stay in the moment and when you stay in the moment, there is no suffering. With the stinging sensation you were aware and totally accepting of the moment. When you can do that then there is no suffering.

If there is no suffering then no grasping at an object has taken place. When there is no grasping at something there is a letting life live, letting it flow. This is called love.

Perfect Masters

A book about to go into the library is called *How to Choose a Guru* by Rick Chapman. It is an A-Z guide designed to help spiritual seekers tell the real from the false. Topics are many and varied. For example, under the letter 'C' are such subjects as Clairvoyance, Compassion and Consciousness, along with a few others. Under 'H' are Healing, Honeymoon and Humility. It was with some interest that I looked under 'M' to see if Meditation was mentioned and, sure enough, the author—who claims to be a seeker himself and not a guru—has dealt with Meditation as well as with Masters (Perfect), Meher Baba, Milarepa, Ministers, Miracles and Money.

What he has to say about meditation is very interesting. He says—correctly—that the Perfect Master does not teach meditation, he teaches love.

Mr Chapman's short essay on meditation contains lots of delightful little gems. He says for example that no meditation can in itself take a seeker to the goal of the spiritual life. He also says of the 'Perfect Master' (a fully enlightened teacher) that he is a 'meditation in himself' and that although he may teach a particular kind of meditation to his followers, he does not regard that meditation as having 'an inherent importance'. He says that such a teacher knows that 'the highest and most effective meditation is love'.

Let me explain what it means to say that the Perfect Master teaches only love.

Have you ever been in love? I do not make the assumption that you have been in love just because you are married or are living with someone. Many people go through their whole lives never having experienced true love. They may well have experienced something which they mistakenly call love but which is more correctly called possessiveness. I will explain what love is and you can decide whether or not you have experienced it.

Imagine that you're a woman and that you fall in love with a man. When you are in that state your mind is completely open; it's soft, it's accepting, it's non-judgemental. If your partner smiles at you, you love it. If he shouts at you, you love it. If he stands on his head and does funny things in the air with his feet, you love it. If he has bandy legs, you don't care, you think they're beautiful anyhow. If he says something nasty and cutting to you it hurts but you bounce back instantly, not with a cutting remark, but with the mind open, soft, accepting of the hurt and only too delighted to be with him, regardless of what he says or does.

When the mind is in love, it registers hurt. It totally experiences hurt. It doesn't deny it. It doesn't squash it out. It experiences it *and* it still stays open and soft. This sort of openness can be seen in a dog. If you have a dog you may have noticed that you can shout at it, swear at it, even kick it and yet it still comes back to you wagging its tail, eyes all soft and gooey, looking up at you adoringly. In spite of your bad temper, the dog returns to you, head lowered a bit, wagging tail tucked in slightly to show submission and clearly hoping you won't shout at it or hit it again. It doesn't get in a huff and say, 'I'm leaving', and run away because you have kicked it. You can mistreat a dog and yet it still stays loyal and responsive and open to you. Some would say the dog 'loves' you. Given my definition of love, I wouldn't quibble with that.

A human being in love accepts anything and everything her partner cares to toss in her direction. As soon as the mind starts to fall out of love then in come the value judgements. 'He shouldn't be like this. He should be different. He should treat me differently. He should get his bandy legs fixed, they're ugly.' No longer does she refer with a laugh to 'his little ways'. No longer does she accept gladly the way he picks his teeth after dinner and the way he gets irritable and shouts at her after he's had too many drinks. No longer does she refer to his 'little ways' in a tone of voice that clearly shows a delight and an acceptance of his particular foibles. Now, his little ways irritate her.

Once the value judgements of what should or should not take place between them creep in, then the voice is harsh, demanding its 'rights'. The mind has closed down; it is no longer open, soft and accepting. No longer does she see her lover as a new and delightful experience every time they meet. Now he is stale, known and confined to a compartment in her mind where she labels him 'Mr Smith, my husband, who looks like this, and behaves like this but who *should* look like this and behave like this.' She's harsh and critical, trying to mould him into an image she can love. Her mind yearns to be soft, accepting and non-judgemental as it was in the early days of their relationship. She feels that if she can only get him to change then she will recapture that love that she once experienced and for which she constantly yearns.

This soft, accepting, non-judgemental state of mind is what the Perfect Teacher is always driving the student towards. The meditation is a technique which assists considerably in the development of this attitude of mind.

Only when the mind is open and accepting as a permanent state does the meditator truly let come in and go out everything from tension to calmness, from turmoil to bliss, from physical well-being to physical pain. Only when the mind is accepting will the meditator allow all the opposites to form and disintegrate, and form and disintegrate again, without making any movement to interfere with the process. Such a state of mind is truly called love.

Love and Inner Wealth

The mind saturated with love fully experiences the opposites; it fully experiences the hurt and the bliss. It is not dulled to them but, at the same time, it makes no movement to interfere with their creation and death. The mind in love is soft, pliant, patient and totally harmless to itself and others.

The mind of love is not concerned to build up possessions, reputation and talents. It does not care to accumulate things, for it knows that its joy rests in being open and free, and in accepting whatever should come along, painful or pleasant. The mind of love is not judgemental; it does not assess its own advantage. The mind of love is free from the idea-of-self in most important respects. Outer wealth means little or nothing to such a mind, for it will regard itself as rich with the full experience of life, no matter what level of physical wealth may be enjoyed. The mind of love is a mind that has untold inner wealth—and that wealth increases and increases the more that it is not sought.

Should anyone try to accumulate inner wealth in the same way as he might attempt to accumulate money or possessions, he immediately becomes poverty stricken in his inner world. It is only possible to have inner wealth by giving it away; by never trying to accumulate it, by never trying to keep it for yourself.

With inner wealth one's horizons are broadened; life becomes a wonderful adventure and greatly satisfying. Inner wealth utterly fills the one-time emptiness felt by those who come to be dissatisfied with the chase after things of the world. Inner wealth is what they have always looked for, although they did not know it, and inner wealth can only be had by refusing to possess anything at all, no matter how many 'possessions' they might have in the world.

The Art of Sacrifice

Sacrifice as a means of spiritual advancement has gone out of fashion now, at least in the more flamboyant forms it used to take. There was a time in history when a wealthy man would sacrifice a percentage of his livestock; he would arrange a great occasion, with priests, with much beating of drums and blowing of horns and with all kinds of ceremonial ritual, and there have many of his horses and cattle put to death.

The art of sacrifice is not entirely dead, however. There are in India today ascetics and holy men who worship Agni, the god of fire. When given a gift, they burn it; they consign it to the holy fire always alight at their side. Onto that fire they throw cloth, paper money and excess food. They sacrifice any gift to the flames.

There are a few of these ascetics in Thailand and one in particular proved to be a great attraction for some of the American GIs who recently occupied that country. The soldiers would take along a gift of gasoline to this crazy old man and watch in delight as it exploded in sacrifice to the fire god. Luckily no one got hurt.

What is the purpose of sacrifice? Is it just some arcane and barbaric custom that has largely disappeared from the world, or does it still go on? Do people still try to placate the gods with sacrifice? Do they still try to avoid incurring their displeasure if they are too rich or too powerful? It seems that if you choose voluntarily to reduce your wealth or to restrict yourself in some way, then there is far less likelihood that the gods will take umbrage as you come close to outdoing them in power and splendour.

Sacrifice is still to be found today. Both commercial companies and private individuals may give away some of their wealth for the benefit of others. Charities are dependent entirely upon the generosity of others. Band Aid raised astounding millions of pounds for famine relief in Africa. There are in existence today whole hospitals which are the result of a single gift by one individual. It all came from sacrifice. The sacrifice of money in a good cause seems to be on another level than killing off horses but in each case the individual is giving up something which is of considerable value to him. He believes it is better to perform a sacrifice than to keep the wealth entirely for himself.

The advantage of sacrifice is quite simply that you feel better about yourself if you do it than if you do not. To give up something that you enjoy or find valuable is a way of making you happier, perhaps even of ensuring your safety and well-being. If you can give up something in a good cause then so much the better, for it means not only do *you* feel better for having made the sacrifice in the first place, but other people are going to feel better as a result of your actions.

Sacrifice, especially of material goods or money, is a way of saying to yourself and to the world at large that you recognise that there are more important things. Sacrifice says that you value more subtle things than the world of possessions and wealth. This attitude promotes psychological health, for it takes away some of the obsession we tend to have with the body and its support in this world.

Forms of Sacrifice

There are many kinds of sacrifice. Whatever you value, that you can sacrifice. You can sacrifice your time, your money, even your health. You can sacrifice anything that is dear to you. You can sacrifice your own freedom of movement, your time on your own, anything that you enjoy. For the best kind of sacrifice, though, it is essential that it should not in any way damage or hurt a living being. In fact you can divide sacrifice roughly into two kinds: that which harms others and that which does not.

Some people work themselves nearly to death and then claim that they have willingly sacrificed themselves. Nothing could be further from the truth in these cases. Sacrifice is not at all the same thing as indulgence. It is not hurting *yourself* by over-indulging in some activity or other. The drug-addict who kills himself with an overdose is not making a sacrifice. The alcoholic who gives up his dignity to beg for another drink is not making a sacrifice. The workaholic, driven by internal need, is not making a sacrifice. To commit suicide is not making a sacrifice. To give up something you do not want is not making a sacrifice. There is much more to it than that.

Who performs sacrifice today? Is it something remote and unusual? Not at all. Parents sacrifice their time, their wealth and their freedom to bring up children to live successfully in the world. Teachers sacrifice their own personal time and inclinations to ensure that their charges learn properly. Nursing staff sacrifice their own comfort in order that others may get well. Soldiers sacrifice their very lives for their country and their countrymen. Those belonging to a church or a temple may sacrifice money and time in its cause.

A Burmese businessman, U Myat Saw, bought a large country house and estate in Oxfordshire for use by others as a meditation centre. He himself was not a meditator or a teacher. He just made available to meditators the buildings and grounds together with the necessary material support to run the place. U Myat Saw was not alone in his sacrifice; his wife cooked all the meals for all those who went to stay, monks and lay people alike. It was only when they realised that people were going there solely for the wonderful Burmese cuisine, with the thought of meditating seriously coming a very poor second, that they stopped supplying food for everyone.

The Benefits of Sacrifice

The benefits of sacrifice are very real. Apart from the possibility of placating the gods, to sacrifice something very definitely lessens one's attachment to it. To lessen attachment is of inestimable value, for all of our troubles are due to that most ugly of mental factors. Attachment is what keeps us bound to the wheel of birth and death. Attachment brings in its wake an inevitable toll of suffering and despair. Attachment is like a traitor, for it seems to promise so much and yet destroys all it touches. Whether the sacrifice is made willingly or with regret, it is always of benefit. There is definite personal advantage in giving up something dear. It is one way of spiritual advancement for those involved in the world.

The Buddha said, 'Looking across the world with the eye of a Buddha, I found none dearer than self.' He found that every living being holds its life very dear. It is the one thing everyone protects as best they can. Sacrifice which kills or harms another being, human or otherwise, steals from him the one thing he values above all else. Such action has extremely painful results and is better avoided. The horse sacrifice or, worse yet, human sacrifice, is without question wrong action, even though done with apparently good motives. The best kind of sacrifice is that which harms neither another living being nor yourself in the process.

Someone making a sacrifice may not be conscious of spiritual values. Sacrifice is often simply a part of life, accepted with little or no understanding of the deeper meanings of the activities that surround it. Often sacrifice is made *because* of attachment and actually strengthens types of behaviour which promote suffering.

Those who do become more conscious of the spiritual dimension of life gradually get interested in various kinds of self-discipline. Finding the benefits from sacrifice to be real, they come to believe that greater self-denial may well hold the key to increasing happiness. This is particularly evident if they should decide to follow a meditative or spiritual path. In this case, one of the first things they learn is to guide their behaviour by a set of rules designed to promote the welfare of the individual and of the community. They learn self-control, a more subtle form of sacrifice.

Self-Control
The opposite of self-control is self-indulgence; the immediate gratification of desires. Self-control in essence is the *restraint of desire for personal gratification*. In the meditative life it is specifically the restraint of those actions which harm other beings in some way.

There is a most important purpose to self-control. It is not merely a question of being tough on yourself so that you can prove that you are better than the next person at being tough on yourself. The purpose of self-control is on the one hand to safeguard the community from individual desires and obsessions and on the other to guard the individual against himself. It allows the human being to resist the lure of temptation and to avoid the paths leading to the downfall.

Worldly downfall occurs when a man or woman gets so tempted by indulgence, power or corruption that they ruin their reputation and career, thus committing professional suicide. I remember one man, very highly placed, who could not resist shop-lifting. The crime itself was not so great, but he was in local government, so he lost his job and all chance at future jobs of a similar kind. This is one danger of lack of self-control.

85

There is another kind of downfall. Indulge enough in action which is based on the gratification of personal desires without thought for the welfare of self or other and you will end up with a bad rebirth. You end up being reborn in circumstances very much worse and more uncomfortable than you currently enjoy.

Types of Self-Control
Self-control is of one kind only in that it is the restraint of desire for personal gratification. In this context most people automatically think of gratification of the desires for food or comfort or sex, but a person can indulge in hatred and anger. These also are desires—desires to hurt or harm other beings. Indulgence in hatred leads to obsession and distress just as surely as does excessive sensual indulgence.

Self-control does have two distinct faces, though. They can be seen by looking at the two 'guardians of the world' of which the Buddha spoke. They are fear of blame and fear of shame. Fear of blame is just as it says, a fear that people will regard you in a bad light if you go against what society considers acceptable at the time. Fear of shame on the other hand is a more internal affair, being of relevance to those who do not care so much what other people think but are much more concerned to live according to their own idea of what is right and proper. Each of these guardians operates only through the exercise of self-control and in no other way. All the laws in the world are implicitly based on the strength of these two.

That applies even to the rules of training that are the foundation of any religious or spiritual way. For example, in the Buddhist way all true seekers try to live by a code of conduct outlined by the five precepts. Initially these may be regarded as laws to be followed. They are in fact much more subtle than that, being a description of the kind of behaviour that prevents the arising of suffering, quite aside from what is currently fashionable.

The five precepts are as follows.
To undertake the rule of training to refrain from:
1. Killing or harming living beings.
2. Taking that which is not given to you.
3. Illegal or inappropriate sexual activity.
4. Lying, slander, gossip and all wrong speech.
5. Indulgence in mind-affecting drink and drugs.

All of these 'rules of training' place some restriction on personal desires common to all people in all walks of life.

The Benefits of Self-Control

Most people exercise self-control. It is hardly possible to live in the world if you do not. However, there is self-control and there is self-control. It is all very well to resist the temptation to steal, for example, but it is quite another matter to attempt always to restrain gossip. Then again, there are three different kinds of behaviour to consider: bodily, verbal *and* mental.

Unless you see some particular point to it, it is difficult always to exercise self-control in these ways. A teacher we know once asked her class what they thought would be the ultimately harmless action. After various suggestions, she gave her idea. It was to sit alone in a room and write a hate-letter—but then never to send it! It was apparent that she did not really consider mental behaviour to be important in the scheme of things.

Those on a spiritual or meditative path endeavour to be impeccable in every aspect of their personal conduct in order to advance in their chosen way. All religious systems, all meditative ways, recognise that self-control is the first major step on the road to truth.

One refinement of self-control is sense restraint. This has extremely beneficial results for anyone engaged in meditation, for it begins to train the mind to look inwards rather than ever-outwards, with corresponding gains in mindfulness, concentration and general understanding.

Self-control is the sacrifice, for the good of others, of one's own desires. Sense restraint is the sacrifice, for one's own welfare, of sensual indulgence. As an aside, have you noticed how, when you do choose not to act on a desire, that desire actually fades away as though it had never existed? This is the one thing that makes the practice of self-control in all its forms into a most rewarding exercise.

There is more to a spiritual way than just self-control, though, even if we do consider the more subtle aspects of it. It is not simply a question of impeccable discipline.

Self-control suffers from one limitation which is not immediately obvious. Being self-controlled, there is no allowance for the unexpected. There is no room for surprise. There is only dedication and effort to restrain, no matter how subtle that restraint has actually become. Self-control is very much a question of manipulating the universe to get what you think you need. As such it prevents the true vision of what is really there.

Surrender
There is another dimension to spiritual practice. Sooner or later all seekers find that constantly looking out for their own advantage begins to seem like an obstacle on the path to true freedom. They begin to believe that their own desire to win is their one major problem.

The spiritual seeker with some experience of meditation and true self-discipline *knows* that there is more to life than his own personal desires, even if those desires are for a closer and closer approach to reality. After all, he has found that desires, left unattended, simply fade away with a corresponding lessening of the sense of disease that was there before. The trouble is that it seems impossible to stop the desires arising in the first place—and this begins to look most unsatisfactory.

Gradually there grows a desire to give up desire. There comes into existence a desire to give up altogether the struggle to control not only the meditation practice but also every aspect of the life-style. The recognition that there is in fact nothing more that you can do; that it all goes on in spite of what your individual desires might say, that it all happens without your permission, makes the idea of doing nothing very attractive. Instead of self-control, self-*surrender* begins to look like a very sensible alternative.

There is the recognition that the world does not need me or anyone else to manipulate and organise it. It runs quite well by itself—and that includes the inner universe of the mind as well as the outer. Feeling this so strongly, there comes the time when the true seeker feels the need to surrender utterly to reality. He wants no more of his own petty manipulations. He wants only to be enveloped in the mantle of truth and freedom. He wants to be at one with all of nature and all of the spiritual world.

What is Surrender?
Surrender is not something negative. It is important to distinguish it from simply 'giving up' because you feel that any effort is not worthwhile. Surrender is positive—a leaning towards the infinite. Giving up, on the other hand, always implies some kind of despair and negativity.

Surrender is unique in that it is based completely in the confidence that everything happens for the best and not for the worst. It is to allow the due processes of life to go on without even subtle manipulation or disturbance. It is to accept that whatever happens to you is very much 'right as it is' and can only be in your best interests in the long term, no matter how painful it might be in the present. All of this is quite different from lying down and giving up because you are not getting your own way.

Surrender is only possible out of a position of strength. Surrender is only possible for those who are disciplined and self-controlled. It takes great courage and dedication to surrender. It cannot be done by the spiritually immature.

It is for this reason that drop-outs and hippies and bums and no-goods are so severely censured. They sometimes claim to be surrendering to the flow of life as it is. Usually, though, they are indulging in what I call 'negative drift'—going nowhere fast. They are completely at the mercy of every wind that blows. Such people may have the right intentions, but it has to be said that they lack the skill and subtlety needed for surrender to work properly. They need training if they are to reap any advantage from what they do.

The purpose of surrender is the quietening of the selfish mind. It is to overcome the tyrannical demands of the personality, with its essentially worldly outlook. Surrender is ultimately to go beyond all the constraints and limitations of the world. Surrender leads finally to enlightenment.

Types of Surrender
Just as there is essentially only one kind of self-control, so too is there only one kind of surrender. The function of surrender is always to eliminate the sense of self. It is to remove the idea that one's own desires are important and should take precedence over those of someone else. Surrender is to give up the false belief that we alone can control our destiny. It is to become truly humble.

Whilst the function of surrender is always to remove the sense of self-importance, the ways in which it manifests are many and varied. Westerners often speak of surrender in romantic terms. Pop song after pop song has the same theme of surrender and romantic love, extolling its virtues endlessly. In complete contrast, the Oriental often first thinks of surrender in mystical or religious terms. In India, particularly, the dominant theme is surrender to a god, or to the highest man can conceive. Indian films, whilst having plenty of 'boy meets girl' interest, are often constructed entirely around the idea of religious or mystical surrender.

Another kind of surrender is that which has to occur at the end of every human life. We all die, without exception. We may, however, have different ideas about how we should go. During the second world war, it was remarked that the

Oriental troops 'died more easily' than those who came from Western cultures. Some people thought this was a Bad Thing. They thought it was somehow not playing the game to give up and die when you were injured. They thought that you should fight to hang on to life at all costs. Others, perhaps the more reflective, were of the opinion that the art of dying easily and gracefully was a rare skill worthy of being cultivated.

How about you? Are you going to be carried off kicking and screaming by the Grim Reaper? Or are you going to learn how to die gracefully, to surrender peacefully, when the time comes?

People Who Practise Surrender
The monk and the nun practise surrender. In the Western tradition, just as in the Oriental, the full-time religious lives a life of poverty, chastity and obedience. In some sects, the newly ordained monk lies prone on the floor whilst his brothers literally walk over him, symbolising the surrender of his own selfish will.

The mystic practises surrender to his god. The bhakti yogin practises surrender of the personal will firstly to his guru and then to reality itself.

On a different level most people practise surrender of the personal will from time to time and in different ways. The employee accepts the commands of the boss. The lover surrenders to the demands of a partner. The artist surrenders to inspiration.

Surrender is an enormously positive process because of the discoveries to which it leads. Surrender leads to a developing trust and faith in the workings of the universe and it leads to greater and greater understanding. Out of the attempts to surrender come many kinds of wisdom.

The Ultimate Surrender
The ultimate surrender is to give up completely the belief in the existence of an independently functioning personal will.

It is to overcome the belief that each of us exists as a permanent, separate and independent entity. At the same time it overcomes the fear of annihilation that troubles so many in the West. The ultimate surrender is accompanied by the realisation of the truth expressed in the old Japanese saying:

When you start on the way, men are men, mountains are mountains and trees are trees. Having gone some way along the path, there are no men, there are no mountains, there are no trees. Coming to the end of the journey, once again men are men, mountains are mountains and trees are trees, *but now no one is confused by the terms.*

The path towards complete surrender very often starts with a vague feeling that it is somehow necessary to sacrifice part of what is dear to you to evade the wrath of the gods. Perhaps it was this kind of feeling that prompted the human sacrifice that seems to have been such a major part of the early civilisations of South America. Even though the direction this sacrifice took is very much to be deplored, the basic desire to sacrifice something is extremely beneficial. Sacrifice can only reduce clinging and attachment.

It is as though we all have a hazy understanding of the way things are, as though each and every one of us has always known the true reality. The absolute 'calls us home' but we have covered up the truth with layer after layer of illusion. The illusion is painful and through the pain and suffering of life our buried intuitions of perfection call to us with insistence. These intuitions filter down through the layers of the mind and get distorted in the process so that we often go wrong. Human sacrifice, sacrifice to the gods of the flesh, sacrifice of human dignity, can all be seen as misguided attempts to do the right thing. It is not so much the *motive* that is wrong, but rather the view of the world.

Gradually we refine our understanding, for we are forever prompted by those hidden intuitions. We never rest until we get it right. Given time and growing wisdom we see that selfish conceit is the problem. Whenever we think that we are somehow a special case separated from the rest of the universe, that is when things go wrong. To sacrifice that selfish concern, to let go of that feeling of personal importance, is the very essence of surrender.

We discover that the art of sacrifice is the same thing as the art of surrender. We find that to learn how to surrender is to learn how to die, whether at the end of a lifetime or from moment to moment. To learn how to die is to learn how to live. Thus the art of sacrifice is the true art of living and contains the secret of true and infinite freedom.

Mental Health

Last summer we were having dinner with some relatives and they asked, more out of mild curiosity than real interest, 'What exactly do you teach?' I thought for a while, wondering how I could present the teaching of the Buddha in a nutshell, for they definitely were not interested in hearing more than that, and also how I could present it in words that would have meaning for two people who had no philosophical or religious background.

I said, 'We teach mental health.' So far so good. I added that nearly every man, woman and child alive is mentally diseased and that we teach a method whereby a person can conquer that disease and become mentally healthy. By now the relatives were looking distinctly uncomfortable and when I added that mental disease usually increases as a person gets older, just as the body degenerates with age, they nearly choked on their dinner—perhaps understandably, as they were both in their sixties.

Mental Disease
The Buddha said, 'I teach but one thing: suffering (*dukkha*) and the cessation of suffering.' One major aspect of dukkha is mental suffering or mental dis-ease. Thus the goal of the

Buddhist way, the cessation of dukkha, is the absence of mental dis-ease, or mental health. Ignorance, craving, hatred, violence, jealousy, envy and resentment are all aspects of mental disease. Freedom from them and their crippling effects is enlightenment and enlightenment is mental health.

In the West we associate mental disease with neurosis, depression, schizophrenia and mental breakdown and accordingly regard the average man, who is not afflicted by these diseases, as normal and healthy. From the standpoint of the Buddha's teaching, it is only the enlightened person who enjoys true mental health; the average man suffers from varying degrees of mental dis-ease.

Only the totally healthy mind, the enlightened mind, can see the full ramifications of dukkha in both its gross form, starving humanity for instance, and in its subtlest forms, such as desiring absolute peace of mind. It is only the healthy mind that sees clearly the utter horror of the diseased mind. It is only the healthy mind that is fully conscious of what a diseased mind actually is and what it feels like, how it's created, how to stop the disease encroaching further and how to swing it round and head it towards health.

The diseased mind, on the other hand, is oblivious of its ill-health. When disease becomes the normal state, the mind does not see it as disease. The mind mistakes the familiar for health and well-being and is completely unaware of its true nature. It's similar to a fish in water. Because the fish is always surrounded by water it has no comparison and is unaware of the true nature of its immediate environment. Remove it, even briefly, from its normal habitat, put it on land, and it becomes aware very forcibly of the *absence* of water.

If you start to meditate and experience consciously, even for a brief moment, the mind concentrated, mindful, buoyant, tranquil and totally absorbed in the now, what you had seen previously as 'normal' you will now regard, by comparison, as very unhealthy.

Work and Mental Problems

A woman had a great deal of upheaval in her life. She had four children and her marriage was in the process of breaking up. She was trying to cope with the divorce proceedings, trying to look after her children, going to court to fight a custody claim by her husband and looking for a new house. The divorce was being delayed because the husband was dragging his heels about money and, on top of all of this, she was also studying for a university degree.

She noticed that when studying all her troubles had to take second place if she was to learn anything. With her strong desire to graduate she pushed down, when she was studying or attending lectures, all the worries, the hatred and the bitterness. When they were pushed down she noticed that the mind was very much sharper and brighter, that she enjoyed life more and that she could cope with and remember more easily all the thousand and one small tasks that had to be done daily to feed, clothe and organise herself and her four children.

She mused that if you had a career that you found really interesting it would so concentrate the mind that you would be happier, therefore mentally healthier, so you wouldn't need to meditate. It seemed to her that an interesting career achieved the same things mentally as did meditation.

Although correct in her observation that concentration does suppress unhappiness, she was wrong about meditation. You still have to meditate in order to experience total mental health. The mind may well be concentrated and happy when working but what happens when you relax? On a few, rare occasions this mother-of-four found, joy of joys, that she had caught up with all her study and her housework. The children were fed and washed and in bed. She could take a few brief moments for herself; she could sit down in her favourite armchair. What happened then? Could she relax? Could she stay sitting there doing nothing and enjoy it? No, she could not. When she 'relaxed', all the worries and problems flooded into her mind.

Work, whether it comes in the form of a career or housework, gardening or building, is a concentration technique. It is a type of concentration meditation (*samatha*) which calms the mind. What you experience when you relax and do nothing or when you sit down and close your eyes to meditate is in fact your *normal* state of mind.

Your Normal State of Mind
What happens for you when you relax or when you sit down to meditate? Are you happy with what you find? Are you bored? Do you experience lots of worry or hatred, or lots of scheming and planning? Whatever you experience most of the time when you are quiet and supposedly relaxing is your natural state of mind. Do you like it?

Going out to work, doing the housework, having a dinner party, reading, watching the television and many more activities all act like a concentration or calming meditation practice. They suppress one's normal mind which is more or less in a state of disease. This fact is acknowledged in homespun philosophy when well-meaning neighbours and relatives give advice to someone who has been through a personal trauma, like a death in the family or a broken relationship. They say, 'Make sure you keep yourself busy, dear. That way the wounds will heal quicker.' Society instinctively recognises—even if it doesn't quite know how it works—that keeping occupied allays negative tendencies.

When someone detests his normal state of mind he will say, 'I have to keep occupied to keep happy.' He can't just sit and relax and enjoy the moment because his mind is not still. As soon as he sits quietly, little hatreds and resentments creep in and chew away in the mind. They work away, polluting, staining, stinking, so that he is driven to rush up to cut the garden hedge, or bake a loaf of bread, or tidy a cupboard—anything to get away from the stink of the mind. It is far better, however, to remove that stink than to run away from it. Diseases have a habit of getting worse if not attended to and cured.

You may have noticed that throwing yourself into activity around the home or at the office just doesn't work on the occasions when the mind is in a really bad state. If the mind is obsessed with some kind of worry about the future, the worry seeps through the barriers that activity can provide and bursts into the mind, taking the attention away from the work you're trying to do.

For example, what happens if you decide to try to get away from severe worry by throwing yourself into digging the vegetable plot? Most of the time your attention will be caught up with going over and over the worry. Before you know it you have dug up by mistake the prize cabbage you've been growing for months to display at the local show. You're so caught up in the worry that you don't even notice what the body is doing.

Keeping occupied to keep the 'nasties' at bay does not work all the time. It's a short-term policy. It will succeed some of the time but it does not work on all occasions. Only facing up to the nasties will totally eliminate them and then only by getting to know what you are doing mentally to bring them about.

Mental dis-ease varies from person to person. Some are mildly afflicted, whilst others are in a very bad state and heading slowly towards chronic and incurable mental ill-health.

Insanity and Senility
The difference between the mental state of the average man and the person society labels as mentally diseased or insane is that the latter's mental ill-health has become extreme almost to the point of no return. Mental disease in those found in mental hospitals has so invaded the mind that it occupies the patient's mental states for most of the day. Such

mental disease is so deep, so strong and so engrained that insight meditation (*vipassanā*) cannot help these people. They are far too ill. They will have to wait for other circumstances—maybe another lifetime—before they can work on establishing true mental health. That is not to say that they cannot establish mental health as interpreted by society. Society's definition of mental health is being able to function in day-to-day activities without causing too much disturbance to those around one. It is quite a different definition to that of enlightenment, the ultimate in mental health as defined by Buddhism. Vipassana meditation works best and only comes to full flowering in those whom society labels as 'mentally healthy'.

If no positive steps have been taken to cultivate mental health a mind may become more diseased as it gets older. Body and mind are inter-linked so that when the body breaks down as it gets older, the mind tends to follow suit. Think of the times when your body is mildly ill, like when you have a cold; doesn't the mind get upset, doesn't it get grumpy? The upset and the grumpiness have their roots in hatred, which is one of the major mental diseases. If you find it difficult to keep calm and collected when the body is mildly ill with a cold, you can imagine what a state you are going to get into when it's fifty or sixty and it's beginning to break down, to get arthritis, backache, heart trouble or cancer.

There is no need for the mind to degenerate just because the body does. It is well within everyone's reach to keep the mind bright, brisk and healthy whilst the body is beginning to break down, gradually and inevitably sliding towards the total collapse of death.

If the mind is coaxed and trained towards health as soon as a person begins to suspect it is diseased, then it will grow daily in health. By the time the body starts to break down with old age, the mind with this training will not be capable of drifting downhill with the body. It will remain bright, alert and fascinated by the changes it observes taking place in a crumbling body and will not be in the least bit distressed by them.

First, though, you have to diagnose the problem. You have to become conscious that you are ill. If a person lives with the illusion that he is healthy when in truth he is mentally diseased then there is no hope. Nothing can be done. He can only sink further and further into mental illness.

Starting to Meditate
A person starts to meditate because he realises that he is not as happy or as fulfilled as he has the potential to be. This is already to acknowledge that he is mentally diseased. He would probably never call it that. He would probably say something like, 'There must be more to life than this.' Identifying this sense of unease, the individual has come to see part of the scope of the Buddha's first noble truth. The Buddha summed up his teaching in four truths, the first of which simply states that there is dukkha; there is suffering, disease, unsatisfactoriness and all manner of problems in the world.

Very soon after you start vipassana meditation it is usual to discover that you seem to be getting worse and worse. One meditator said to me the other day, 'Since I've started this meditation I've become more and more negative.' She was in fact mistaken. The meditation does not and cannot cause a person to become more negative; it does not cause one to become more diseased. It was the ill-health that *already existed* in her mind that she was beginning to observe. Rather than being a depressing sign, it is a very positive indication when a meditator becomes more conscious of the depths to which the mental disease has gone. To have at last correctly diagnosed disease, where one had previously thought there was health, means that now one can start to *do* something about the problem.

The discovery and recognition of mental disease marks the beginning of the journey towards health. Recognising how bad the mental health has always been is regarded by the meditation teacher as a sign of meditative progress. It's also a marvellous discovery for the meditator because it rightly stimulates his or her desire to achieve mental health as a first priority over and above physical health.

The Cause of Mental Disease
Having diagnosed the disease, the question that naturally arises from that discovery is, 'How did I come to be diseased? What causes this mental disease?'

You don't have to be a meditator to realise that it is not possible to remain in a good mood throughout the day from the moment you wake in the morning until your head hits the pillow at night. At some time during the day that good mood is going to disintegrate and be replaced with irritability or annoyance or depression or anxiety. A person who meditates becomes even more aware of just how short-lived are those pleasant states of mind and how much the mind swings back and forth between good and bad moods.

The cause of mental disease is wanting things to be different than they are. Most people wish to be in a good mood all day and every day. Wanting good moods, it follows that they dislike the bad moods. The discomfort and dislike at not getting what you want is suffering, dukkha, as defined in the first noble truth. Wanting something other than what is present in the moment the Buddha called craving. Wanting to be in a good mood rather than in a bad mood is wanting something other than what is present and is therefore craving. The second of the four noble truths declared by the Buddha states that craving is the cause of mental disease.

The Control of Mental Disease
A meditator complained saying, 'Even though I'm aware that I hate my bad moods and want only pleasant states, I

can't seem to do anything about it.' This man's problem is a lack of commitment to the spiritual path, which is another way of saying that he lacks commitment to mental health. He claimed that he could not 'switch on' commitment just because he had decided he should be committed. Is he correct in his assumption or does he have more options than he is aware of?

How does a smoker give up smoking? One day he decides, 'Today I will give up smoking.' Twenty years of smoking can be abandoned with that one decision. It doesn't take a further twenty years to undo the habit. It takes just one moment—one decision. Whether the person actually succeeds at giving up smoking with that one thought will depend on how strong his determination is and that in turn will depend on how much desire there is not to smoke.

A person gives up smoking for a variety of reasons. He may give it up because it's affecting his breathing or because it's anti-social or because it may seriously damage his health in the future or because he can no longer afford it. One could say that a smoker gives up the habit because he sees it as damaging his health, whether it be his physical or financial health. He desires health and that desire grows and grows until one day he says, 'Today I'm finished with smoking.'

The involvement with smoking does not just end with that one thought, however. If he has been a heavy smoker he will have withdrawal symptoms. He will have recurring unpleasant physical and mental feelings, as well as frequent thoughts of, 'Oh, if only I could have just one cigarette.' He will be irritable and short-tempered. He knows that one puff on a cigarette will end all his agony.

What does he do? If his *vision* of himself as a healthier person as a result of giving up smoking is strong and burning in his mind then he will be aware of all the physically uncomfortable feelings and the constant nagging thoughts about having a cigarette but he will not act on those feelings or those thoughts. He will just keep directing his efforts towards his mental picture of himself as a healthier person.

That picture is a concept. It is a dream. It is a vision of a possible future. The smoker makes use of that dream to work himself up to the point where he can decide to give up smoking. He continues to use that dream to ensure that he doesn't backslide and give in to unpleasant feelings and suddenly start smoking again.

He can only be said to have actualised his picture of himself as a healthy being once the unpleasant physical feelings have completely died away and he no longer thinks about having a cigarette. This occurs when his physical system has eliminated all the toxins accumulated from the smoking. He will be able to breathe better and walk up hills without puffing. He will feel fitter and financially better off. This can take as long as eight months, during which time he is always in danger of falling back into the habit because the physical and mental patterns that were set up with the act of smoking have not yet closed down and been deactivated.

Once those habit patterns have been closed off then it can be said that the smoker has arrived at, and is fully established in, his vision of physical health. He is no longer in danger of backsliding into smoking.

During those very trying months the smoker is sustained in his determination not to smoke firstly by his dream of himself as a non-smoker and secondly by the various disciplines he undertakes to help himself actualise his vision. He undertakes these commonsense disciplines so as not to allow the craving for a cigarette, which he knows still lurks under the surface, to be satisfied.

These disciplines include rules like not having cigarettes in the house, not lingering in front of a shop which sells cigarettes but passing quickly by, not frequenting pubs where the air is blue with cigarette smoke, not mixing much with his smoking pals. If he does put himself into environments where cigarettes are easily available it will be only a matter of days before he's back to the smoking habit once again.

The Vision of Mental Health

We can draw a parallel between the smoker who is unsuccessful at giving it up and the meditator who is aware that cravings and hatreds are the cause of his ill-health, but whose addiction to craving prevents him from committing himself to mental health. We can see just what the uncommitted meditator has to do in order to ensure that he reaches mental health.

All of you here meditate. You might like to examine your own commitment to see if it is as strong as it needs to be for the best results.

Firstly, you need to take a look at your vision. What is it and is it burning brightly? Each one of you has a vision of what you expect to become if you meditate. Broadly speaking, you have a vision of yourself as a healthier being. You may see yourself as healthier in terms of being more aware of your inner universe, or more fulfilled, or happier with yourself, or fully understanding how the different aspects of life fit together. Whatever form your vision takes it will involve picturing yourself mentally healthier than you are at this very moment.

That vision is important. It is important that it exists and it is important that it is clear and strong and very appealing to you. It is important that you turn your mind to it often, that you think about what form it takes and that you refine the details. In short, it is important to redefine your vision at frequent intervals.

This vision of mental health, this dream, is your idea of enlightenment. It is your interpretation of the third noble truth which the Buddha defined as the cessation of suffering. Without a vision of enlightenment you would not bother to meditate at all. It is that vision of future mental health which keeps you driving on and on, through all the difficulties of the path, through the low periods when you would love to abandon meditation, Dhamma-study and everything connected with assisting you to actualise your vision. Your vision is your guiding star, lighting your way, beckoning to you. It is the thing that keeps you going.

Ironically, your vision of mental health is bound to be inaccurate. If it were accurate you would be enlightened. It is for this reason that it is important to redefine your vision from time to time. If your vision is too inaccurate it will actually stop you from making your dream a reality. The more closely your dream of mental health matches the real state of mental health, the more appealing will that dream be to you and the easier you will find it to walk the meditative path.

The Commitment to Mental Health

A meditator becomes committed to mental health dependent upon the strength of his vision of enlightenment. Once his vision of reaching the peak of mental health has become strong, so strong that he wants it more than anything else in the world, then commitment to that vision automatically switches on.

Commitment is action. Action is commitment. If you say you want to do something but do not act, you are not in fact committed, no matter what you say. For example, if you decide to get up and walk across the room but, instead, stay sitting in the chair, you have not committed yourself to walking across the room. You have only *thought* about committing yourself to it. If you decide to practise mindfulness of body and think, 'I will be conscious of the body getting out of this chair and I will be conscious when it is fully upright' and then you let the mind wander to worries about the day ahead whilst the body's going through the motions, you are not committed to the action of mindfulness or awareness. You have not followed through the *intention* to be mindful with the *act* of mindfulness and so you are not committed to mindfulness. The action you made was to worry. You are in fact committed to the act of worry and not to mindfulness, which is to say that you are at that time committed to mental disease and not to mental health.

106

After some initial training a meditator is likely to say, 'I'm aware that I'm full of hatred (or sluggish and sleepy, or worrying) but I'm incapable of stopping it. I keep falling into the same old mental habit patterns. I don't seem to be able to do anything about it.' This early conclusion is drawn in error for although the meditator's statement acknowledges that things are conditioned, it fails to acknowledge the conditioning, active nature of many of the mental processes.

Conditioning is the deliberate action you make *now* by your own choice. If a person says, 'I'm the worrying kind' it implies that the mind, from past habit, naturally *inclines* towards 'chewing things over'. In other words, the mind is conditioned or predisposed towards worry as a mental behaviour pattern. What is not clearly seen is that the person then *chooses* to worry right now, in the present. He has to choose to worry rather than, say, choosing to turn the mind towards being conscious of bodily movement.

The mind just does not worry by itself. It has to choose to worry about something after an object has been presented to one of the senses. For example, if you see a mental picture of yourself losing your job, that picture will be accompanied by a feeling, in this case probably a very unpleasant feeling. The following moment is the moment of action or conditioning. It is the moment of commitment. You choose either to worry about that picture of yourself losing your job, which is to choose mental ill-health, or you choose not to worry but instead to turn the mind to something neutral or positive. This latter course of mental action is healthy, for it avoids commitment to the negative. You may choose to attend to bodily movement, which is skilful action and leads to mental health, or you may choose to act by keeping the mind still and watching the picture and the feeling fade away, which also leads to mental health.

In every case you actually do *choose*; you either choose the healthy path or you choose the diseased path. You exercise commitment always. It is up to you to select the direction that commitment will take. Systematic observation of the mental processes will show you that you are kidding yourself if you think the mind worries by itself and that you have no control over it.

Building a Mental Shield
Having a strong vision is in itself not the whole answer. You need a shield to protect yourself from the 'enemies' you meet whilst journeying towards mental health.

The framework of the shield consists of a variety of self-imposed disciplines. These will include the precepts (ethical rules of training) for the layman or the more inclusive *vinaya* rules for the monk or nun. They may include additional rules as your meditation teacher directs. Even though these rules appear to be imposed from without, you still have to choose whether you abide by them or not. To that extent, they are in fact self-imposed.

Besides the disciplines, the shield also consists of concentration and wisdom. Wearing a shield on your arm made up of these three—discipline, concentration and wisdom—is all you need to protect yourself. The shield includes all the factors you need to walk the path to eventual mental health. With self-discipline you are guarded from your own weaknesses. With concentration you can focus the mind sufficiently to see what kinds of mental behaviour patterns you yourself have developed over the years. With wisdom you can come to see what needs to be done to come to perfect mental health. The shield is a simile for the eightfold path of Buddhism which the Buddha described in the last of the four noble truths. He said that not only does there exist the cessation of all suffering (the third truth) but also there is a definable way, the eightfold path, by following which it is possible to come to the complete cessation of suffering.

Enemies to Mental Health
Enemies to mental health are things like ill-will, sensual desire, restlessness, worry, anxiety, laziness and many more. In Buddhism they are personified as Mara (the Tempter)

and his daughters. They line the road you are walking along and they tempt you from the right path. Are you not terribly tempted by sloth after a delicious meal or by ill-will when accused of something you haven't done? These enemies, Mara and his daughters, come from within you. You create them. They are the ways you choose to respond to life.

You start your journey to mental health by becoming aware that there is a lot of hatred, worry, resentment, guilt or depression constantly affecting the mind and you become aware that you don't want them. You realise you don't want all these nasties but want something other, something better. You then conceive a vision of a healthy mental state that never disappears or dies. The stronger that vision is, the more you want it. Once you really desire it strongly, you become committed to mental health. You commit yourself by making actions in the form of discipline, concentration and wisdom. These three combine to make your vision a reality.

The Way to Mental Health
A woman who had obviously been thinking about meditation, what benefits it would have for her and what it would involve her in, said one day, 'If I meditate, I don't want it to take over my life. I still want to play with my children, go to concerts, talk with friends. I just want it to be something added to my life. I don't want it taking over because it does do that for some meditators, doesn't it? They don't want to do anything else but meditate.'

It was pointed out that meditation has to become the main focus of your life if it is to work. It *has* to dominate every breathing hour. You need to become obsessed with meditation—but meditation is not just sitting on your backside with your eyes closed.

If you are cooking the evening meal, meditation is actually being there with the cooking. It is not thinking about what you are going to cook tomorrow or resenting the harsh words that passed between you and your partner earlier in the day, wishing you hadn't said them and going over and over the whole event. Meditation is keeping the attention on the cooking, letting there be just the action of cooking. Meditation is being aware of the movement of the body to pick up ᴜᴇ cooking ingredients and of the movement of the body as it places them in the frying pan.

Meditation is the noticing of smell as fragrance lifts into the air when the ingredients hit the sizzling fat. It is the noticing of the sounds of frying. It is the noticing of stray memories of past conversations flitting through the mind, not grabbing at them and then becoming obsessed with anxiety about them, but letting them come into mind and float through. Meditation is the returning of the attention to the movement in the arm as it stirs the ingredients in the frying pan.

All this is keeping the attention on cooking. This is living in the moment and allowing there to be only cooking. Meditation is not to have your body set on automatic and to let it do the cooking whilst your mind is off planning and fretting about tomorrow.

When you are cooking, let your mind *and* body cook. That way there is no separation. That way you are meditating properly.

Commitment to Meditation
When it is explained to would-be meditators that this is the true meaning of letting meditation dominate your life, they are invariably happy. Most wrongly imagine that allowing meditation to become your main focus would mean giving up family and job and becoming a recluse, then sitting on a chair with eyes closed all day and all evening. Nothing could be further from the truth. This is not meditation. Meditation is being fully, mind and body, in the moment. It is not wishing to be anywhere else or have anything else present other than what is being experienced here and now.

A healthy mind is one that works when work is required to be done and is fully attentive to the task in hand. When there is no work to be done a healthy mind sits quietly, enjoying the silence, and is totally immersed in doing nothing.

In order to stop constantly being caught up with plans, schemes, dreams about the future, or thoughts, regrets, longings for the past, one has to train the mind. It is easier, less of an uphill struggle, if it is trained when the body is inactive and quiet. It is easier to train the mind when the body is seated on a chair in a relaxed and disciplined manner, with the eyes closed and far away from distractions like people, telephones and doorbells. It is not so easy to keep the mind in the moment when the body is active, when shopping perhaps, or arguing with the kids, but it does become easier to do when active if the mind has been adequately trained through the initial seclusion of the sitting practice.

If daily living is to become for you zestful, fresh and alive regardless of what is happening, regardless of whether you are experiencing your own marriage ceremony or the death of someone close, then you need to work at developing mental health. You need to take up meditation.

Creating the World You Want

Do we actually live in the same world as our fellow beings? We perceive things differently from one another and I think we have to say that the worlds we inhabit are therefore quite different. There is a superficial agreement that, for example, we experienced the sunshine today, but not one of us saw exactly the same thing. Not one of us felt the same thing. Not one of us heard the same thing. How then can we say that the world we were living in during the day was the same as that of our companions? It seems that we can only agree on the broad outline of events and even then only with difficulty. Consider how many different views of the world there are, even in general terms.

Some look at the world as a whole and see only struggles for political power, like the freedom fighters in Afghanistan or the students in South Korea. They see nation fighting against nation, oppressor against oppressed, poor against rich, race against race.

Others see everything in terms of abundance or lack of natural resources. Their concerns are not with politics, except perhaps in a very peripheral way, but with man's use of his environment. Their world consists of quite different things. It consists of tropical rain forests and blue whales, fossil fuel reserves and alternative technology, famine and flood, starvation and natural disaster.

Yet others scarcely perceive these things at all; they are concerned only with accounts receivable and credit control, with the latest hit single or album release, with the baby's nappy-rash and what to cook for dinner. Their world consists of getting the car serviced and the price of petrol, wall-papering the dining room, and trying to feel happy about the in-laws coming over at the weekend.

All of these worlds are quite different and, to complicate matters further, each of those who inhabits these different worlds will perceive them in a different way. If you ask ten different people who attended the same event what they experienced you will get ten different versions. Each one perceived it quite differently from the others. The event impinged on his or her consciousness quite differently from any of the other nine people present. Did they see the same thing? Definitely not. Are their worlds the same?

When it comes to personal experience—and is not all experience *personal* in the end?—then we have to say that each of us lives in a unique world. The world each of us perceives is uniquely his own. It is secret from other people and we cannot actually communicate it to them. Even if our communication skills are excellent, what we say will be interpreted by each person in his or her own unique way—and we still have totally different worlds.

This separation and uniqueness originates in the nature of the senses and in the way we have been conditioned to view the world. The senses can catch only a fraction of what is really going on out there, whatever it is. We long for true contact with others and deeper recognition than it seems we can actually get. We find ourselves constantly frustrated in our desires to 'pull it all together', for the sense of separateness does not go away. Indeed, the harder we try to merge with life the more we become conscious of our separation from it. This is the suffering that the Buddha spoke of so eloquently. This is Samsara, the round of suffering, the round of birth and death.

Buddhist teaching at the conventional level tells us that we have many lifetimes; that we are born now here, now there, as we continue life's journey. It tells us that all deliberate actions have a result in the future. It tells us further that, until we develop true wisdom, we keep going round and round the worlds of birth and death, forever seeking satisfaction and trying to avoid pain, and reaping the results of what we have done before.

Lessons to Learn

We are all faced with the identical problem, even though the worlds we inhabit are so very different. Everyone is conscious of something missing, something wrong. It is as though we are literally stumbling around in the dark trying to find what we need to be happy. In a very real sense we are all on the same journey together; the journey towards completeness, fulfilment and freedom. As we eventually discover, it is a journey towards the discovery that we have never ever been anything but perfect and that the light of truth was only temporarily obscured by the darkness of false ideals and dreams.

The journey towards freedom, Nibbana, is our one and only task. In each lifetime the personality manifests certain strengths and weaknesses. The task of this personality is to learn certain specific lessons about 'life, the universe and everything' and thus to remove some of the blindness with which it is afflicted.

From this point of view this world of ours is an enormous school with about four billion pupils. Everyone who is born has lessons to learn about the blindness with which he is afflicted. That blindness takes the form of a fundamental ignorance of the true nature of life and is the root cause of all suffering and distress in all the worlds.

Just like any school there are pupils in all grades. Some know next to nothing, being unaware even that they are in school. Others, the seniors, know all of the different classes and levels within the school and already have some knowledge of what they will do when they leave. They know, too, that it is only possible to leave the school once all the lessons have been learned properly. No one can fool the examiners or cheat in any way for the final judge is yourself and you always know, deep down, the truth of things as they are.

Where do we go wrong in our efforts to find freedom and perfection? Where do we miss the point when we try to find our ultimate satisfaction?

We cling to things, ideas and situations that are no longer appropriate for us. It is as though a grown man were to insist on carrying with him everywhere the teddy-bear he had as a child. Such behaviour is not adult. It tells us that the man, although grown to full physical stature, is still a baby in all important respects. He has not learned properly the lessons of life.

We make mistakes on our journey to perfection when we try to resist change or when we try to hasten it. When we grasp strongly at something—whether it be a teddy-bear or another person, a possession or a fixed idea—then we suffer the torture of dukkha, suffering, as we attempt to force reality to satisfy our own personal craving or hatred. We make these efforts in an attempt to feel safe and secure, in an attempt to gain fulfilment and freedom from pain, or to ward off fear and anxiety.

Creating the World

Every person lives in a unique world. That world is constructed from moment to moment and is only very loosely based on 'the real world'. Think for a moment of the problems experienced by the paranoid schizophrenic. He is *convinced* that people are seeking to damage or destroy him. This knowledge and the perceptions that go to support it form a major part of his waking experience. It is not possible simply to tell him that he is mistaken, for everywhere he sees 'proof' that he is right in his assumptions.

What of ordinary people who are not suffering from this kind of disorder? How do they see their worlds?

I used to travel by underground train to and from work each day. Some mornings the people with whom I travelled seemed rough and uncouth, ugly and twisted, bitter and hateful. It looked as though all of the really stressed and disadvantaged had chosen the same carriage in which to ride. It was like being in a travelling freak show or mental asylum and sometimes seemed quite dangerous.

On other mornings, though, there used to be quite a different set of people on the train. These people were carefully dressed and carried themselves with a sort of weary pride. Their faces were noble and shining, reflecting a quiet confidence in life and a consciousness of purpose. Some of them looked a little care-worn, not unnaturally, but all seemed to be happy with the sacrifices they were having to make to earn the money to keep themselves or their families alive. I felt privileged to travel with *these* people and the day would start well on that account.

It used to puzzle me. Why were there two so different sets of people? I pondered and investigated the problem for weeks. I did not always travel at exactly the same time so I made a careful mental note of the times of day when each set would appear. 'Baddies' at 08.39, 'Goodies' at 08.42, and so on. That did not seem significant. Was it the actual day? 'Weirdos' on Mondays, 'Straights' on Tuesdays? That did not work either. Theories of time-warps, atmospheric pressure variations and the phases of the moon all followed one another into oblivion.

I ran out of theories and the problem was still there. Sometimes I would travel with the 'Uglies', sometimes with the 'Aristocrats'. There *had* to be a reason. There was. It was so simple that when I saw it everything went still and quiet. The two sets of people were, in a very real sense, my creation. When I was in a dark and evil mood I perceived my world as populated by dark and evil people. When my mood was light and laid back, happy and confident, I peopled my personal world with angels and beings of light. That is where

117

the two groups came from. I created them. I created my own world—all the time.

All of us continually create the universe in which we live, eat and breathe. Whatever there may be out there, the things and events we perceive are created by us out of our expectations, moods, hopes and fears. To say that the things that we create are not real is to miss the point. We treat them as if they were—and therein lies the difficulty.

Visualisation and Mental Reinforcement
We see the world in a certain way. We actually visualise our environment and, as we do so, it becomes true for us. Now some people think that they cannot visualise, that they are verbal rather than visual people, but let me assure you that everyone does in fact visualise their environment, internal and external, and thereby keep it in being. I would like you to try the following exercise.

Close your eyes and imagine yourself in a room in which you spend a lot of your time and therefore know well. It might be the kitchen or the office. See if you can remember where the major pieces of furniture are in relation to the doors and windows. Do you remember leaving any papers or magazines on the working surfaces, whether kitchen table or office desk? Can you remember what's in the fridge or the desk drawers...?

Most of you I'm sure were able to remember most of those things without difficulty. Whatever it was that you did to remember, that *for you* is your way of visualising. It does *not* have to be three-dimensional. It does not have to be in vivid technicolour. Whatever you did to remember those things is perfect visualisation. You do not need to develop the skill. You already have it.

Continuous Creation
Our powers of visualisation make objects appear every moment. We actually create them as we visualise. Every

person has a stream of habitual mental activity (*sankhāra khanda*) running through the mind.

This mental activity and commentary is composed of visions and words, pictures and comments about the state of your own personal world; the world you create by just this very process. The objects in your world do not appear by themselves. You create them. You bring them into existence. You are the architect of your entire universe, all the time.

For example you visualise your 'self', using exactly the same methods as you use to visualise a room you know, but in this case you add to the bare facts all kinds of dubious extras arising out of judgements and comparisons. In this way you actually *see* yourself as ugly and unworthy or as superior and beautiful. You create (that image of) yourself by your own visualisation skills—which we *all* have.

Think of a piece of movie film. It has countless successive pictures or frames which are run past the projector lens at a rate of about twenty-five a second. Each picture is still and has no movement in it at all. Each one is nearly the same as the one before. Looking at individual frames is not very exciting but when the film is projected then everything changes dramatically; there is life and movement and there appear to be real people and objects in front of you. This is continuous creation. Out of a series of separate sense impressions we create something that was not there in the first place.

What happens when you get into difficulties with meditation? You sit down with an expectation of how it will go. Expecting pain you are not at all surprised when you feel a twinge in your back. Looking at it you decide that it could get worse, if you are not careful. You look at it some more and, sure enough, it shows definite signs of setting in for the hour. Now you are conscious of it as a background to all other efforts. You begin to worry about the time. Will you be able to stand it, especially if the pain increases—which it seems to be doing? You look at it again and now it is really burning and cutting into you. Frame by frame, picture by picture, you are creating a personal world of pain and worry...

Sometimes you sit down to meditation and you feel good. You really do not have any particular expectations and when you do feel a twinge in your back you think, 'There's a bit of residual tension letting go. Thank goodness I have an hour in which to relax physically. The body will be all smoothed out by the end of the session.' This meditator builds quite a different world—still using the same techniques of visualisation, but this time in a positive and useful way.

Continuous Change
Continuous creation of this kind holds a message of enormous hope for everyone who would wish to change themselves for the better. Every new creation supplants whatever was there before; it is a new picture, a new event, a new reality. The old image, whatever it was, utterly disappears. In fact it is truly the case that nothing lasts; everything is disappearing into oblivion with every instant.

You do not have to destroy anything, for there is in reality nothing to get rid of—anything that appears then disappears so quickly that it is not possible to destroy it. Your task is rather to create a harmonious and sensible attitude to your own personal world and thereby to alter your way of seeing. You have to alter the way in which you visualise the world. You have to change your mental monologue which creates the world, not the world itself.

If we could train ourselves to imagine only the things we really want; if we could train ourselves to think positive and uplifting thoughts, then the world in which we find ourselves would be as perfect as it is possible to be. It is true that we need to know something of the way the universal laws function—it is no good wishing always to cling to security or happiness, for example, for there is no way that these things can last—but with diligence and effort it is possible to make the most revolutionary changes in one's own personal world—and what other world is there?

It is not enough to learn about these things. We have actually to put them into practice if we are to graduate to the next class in the school we have chosen to attend. The personality has to learn these things as behaviour patterns rather than intellectual knowledge. Only then will they become 'second nature' as time goes by.

It is here that the analogy begins to break down for to speak of school suggests that there is an organisation of school masters and mistresses who direct us and help us to learn. Spiritual guides are few and far between. For most people, life itself is the teacher. Only if we ourselves are alert to the lessons she has to teach will we improve our understanding. It is up to us to observe and to try and find the links, the connections between things, so that we may discover the laws of the universe. We have to develop and maintain an attitude of enquiry. It is not enough simply to suppose that the answers will come of their own accord. Each of us has to do the work and, if we get it right, we stand a chance of freeing ourselves from all our burdens.

There are of course obstacles to learning but they too are self-produced. When something important occurs you usually get tense. You try either to hold on to the moment or to reject it. You try to stop 'good' things disappearing or you try to stop 'bad' things from coming into existence. In short, you resist. You resist natural and inevitable change.

If you have something like pain in the meditation, you resist it. You attempt to prevent the natural flow of things. You grasp at *your idea* of how things should be and in that attempt you create a mental pattern of resistance which affects not only the present moment but also future, similar moments. You condition yourself to tighten up, to grasp, every time you experience a problem.

The distillation of this experience becomes your new personality and will eventually affect future lives as well as this one. We create all our problems in life because of grasping and attachment. We grasp at pleasure or pain and create for ourselves a problem which we then have to solve. And so it goes, round and round.

Growing in Wisdom
If we could learn our lessons properly we would cease to grasp at things, people or events, whether pleasant or painful, and life would take on a very different aspect from that which we normally perceive.

Sometimes it does happen. Sometimes we do feel on top of the world and not threatened by anything. Sometimes we are surrounded by angels rather than demons and life is sweet. Then we are not concerned to try to halt the flow of life. We let things come and go as they please. We form no particular judgements about people or events. Everything seems perfect.

But it does not last. We cannot maintain such an enlightened attitude for very long. Before we know where we are, the sky has gone black and we are once again in dark despair and cannot remember the lighter times—just as it seems impossible in the depths of winter that the world will ever be warm again. Summer seems like an impossible dream.

What is wrong? Why can't we hold on to our better times? Why do we oscillate all over the place and lose our way so easily?

The answer is simple. We do not *know* the nature of the world we inhabit. We do not know what is 'really real' and what is mere imagination. We do not know what we can do and what we cannot do. We have to find out all these things before we can solve the problem of existence. We have to enquire of our own experience to see what really is happening. Only then will we stop wavering and gain some stability and security.

Learning to Let Go
We can learn to let go fully by coming to see that there is really nothing to grasp at (except a mistaken idea) in the first place. Careful and systematic examination of all aspects of our experience, internal and external, will begin to show that nothing lasts in the way that most people think it does. In fact close observation will show that nothing lasts at all, being formed as it is out of fleeting sensory impressions. This is what the meditation on impermanence (*anicca*) is all about; it is designed to break down the habit of grasping.

If nothing lasts at all, where are all the things we thought to exist? What has happened to them? In truth, they never were there. We had just assumed that they existed in that relatively permanent form. In reality there is nothing to grasp at for even as you become aware of a sensory impression it has already gone. The word *anicca* should never be translated as 'change': it is 'impermanence'. Nothing whatsoever that we create or visualise can last. There is actually no *thing* to change. There is only impermanence.

Seeing this fact of transience, even partially, it becomes impossible to grasp so strongly at your own advantage and as you cease to fight against reality so strongly, life becomes fuller and richer and very much more worthwhile.

World Peace
You sometimes hear of people who are working for world peace. They work tirelessly to feed the starving, to heal the sick and to bring harmony to those torn by war and unrest. But what does world peace really mean? How could it come about?

The evidence of millennia is that world peace in the outer, so-called objective sense is at best a worthy dream and at worst a foolish fantasy. If world peace is to be established it cannot be 'out there'; it must be an internal matter. It must be a question of establishing peace within *one's own*

123

world—which is as we have seen the only one each of us has.

Herein lies the wisdom of the practice of loving kindness which, when properly developed, is practised to all beings in the world—one's own world. If world peace is to be found, it will be only here, nowhere else. World peace is essentially a personal matter which at the same time embraces all-there-is.

Looking at the world in this way makes a great deal of sense of the bodhisattva vow—something that has puzzled many people keen to become enlightened as soon as possible.

Anyone taking the bodhisattva vow promises among other things to put aside thoughts of his own enlightenment until 'all beings in the world are freed'. What does this really mean? Where are 'all beings in the world'? Are they not in fact created in the mind of the personality by the very processes of visualisation and thinking that we have been talking about? In which case the question of freeing all beings in the world is simply(!) a question of freeing all beings in one's own *personal* world—and immediately becomes a real possibility rather than a charming fantasy.

Beings—self or other—are created by the self-same visualisation techniques and mental commentary that everyone practises on a constant basis. The problem is not so much the fact that it goes on but rather that, in our ignorance, we believe implicitly in the permanence of the things thus created. When we come to see the truth—that none of these created things, whether objects or people, is in any way a lasting thing but is rather a series of images with no substance—then it becomes impossible for us to grasp at and be attached to any of them.

From that moment on we drop the burden of creation, we drop all attachment and grasping, we stop trying to create perfect personal circumstances for we know that, really, there is nothing to create. There is simply what is—and none of it is ever static in any respect whatsoever. This is true freedom and it is what is meant by 'going beyond the world' for, at this level of understanding, there is no longer any world. Nothing is seen as fixed and lasting. Nothing is seen as 'me' or 'mine'. Nothing is craved for and nothing is hated. All ignorance has disappeared as though it never existed—and all is well, now and forever.

This is why the enlightened person is never reborn: there are no more lessons to learn. He or she has graduated from the school of life and needs to take no more classes or examinations. The task is done. The journey is ended.

The Many Faces of Death

Tonight's talk is centred round a personal story: the story of my mother's last two weeks of life. It's about how she coped with her approaching death, and how the family, relatives and friends coped. It is a typical story—the reactions, the fears, the anger and the embarrassments suffered by those who were close to her are common to most people who suddenly find themselves facing death—and because it is a typical story, it illustrates well the many faces of death, which is why I have chosen to tell it to you in some detail.

This account is for those who have been exposed to death and have found it an embarrassing and difficult experience, and it is for those who have not yet been exposed to death and want to know what to do when the occasion arises. It is also for those meditators who in answer to the question, 'Why do you want to meditate?' have said, 'Because I want to learn how to die properly.' Death is one experience that all human beings have in common; we all know that sooner or later it will be our turn to die.

Some of us share in the dying experience many times throughout life because we are present at the death of many people. Others of us face this experience only once, when we ourselves arrive at the doors of death.

The Face of Terror

One of the faces of death, a very common one, is the terrified face. It is the face seen by those who have ignored death throughout their lives and who have refused point blank either to talk or to think about death, regarding the subject as morbid and one which, if indulged in, would hasten their own deaths. This superstitious attitude is a common human failing, as is ignore-ance of anything found unpleasant or threatening.

We ignore all sorts of things which we find frightening. We ignore our own anger, our own worries, our own fears and our own violence, believing that by refusing to acknowledge these dark and fearful things they will somehow disappear. Only when we are prepared to start learning do we discover that looking squarely at something, whether it be our own anger or our own death, transforms that thing into another experience entirely, one which is no longer fearful and terrifying but is instead enriching and beautiful. We discover that ignoring these dark and ugly qualities actually makes them grow stronger.

The Angry Face

Death has an angry face. It is aroused by the question, 'Why me?' The dying person is angry that he is dying. This can be seen particularly in the terminally ill with about six months left to live.

Anger also grips the members of the family. They feel helpless and can't see any purpose in their loved one lying on the bed, in physical and mental pain, unable to wash himself, or turn himself, or feed himself. To family members, those last weeks look futile, painful and degrading, and so they get angry with frustration. The angry face of death comes and goes in waves for both the dying person and the onlookers. I have seen family members get angry, friends get angry and even nurses get angry though they have been employed to nurse the dying person for only one day.

The number of times the angry face presents itself is directly linked to spiritual development. Anger surfaces frequently and with great intensity when there is no knowledge of what happens after death, no knowledge of how the dying process works, no knowledge of action (*kamma*) and result (*vipāka*), and no experiential knowledge of conditionality. When one has a deep and experiential understanding of these things, then anger doesn't even flicker across the mind.

For some people the spiritual path does not include the concepts of rebirth, kamma or conditionality but does contain a belief in the will of God. These people say, 'Whatever happens, whether it be pleasant or painful, it is God's will. Therefore it is right that this illness and dying are happening to me. The degree to which I can accept what is happening with total surrender and no questioning, the degree to which I am successful at this surrendering, indicates the degree to which I am fulfilling God's will.' As long as this is not just a pretty religious concept but is a basic, conscious attitude which permeates his whole being, there will be no anger for the dying person or for the onlooker with this attitude. Surrender to God's will incorporates the ideas of action-and-result and conditionality and therefore the person who surrenders ends up with spiritual benefits similar to the Buddhist whose every fibre is saturated with understanding of rebirth, kamma and conditionality.

There is far less grief and far less crying when a dying person or an onlooker to the death process has a deep conviction that there are other realms besides the human one. They expect, after death, either to be reborn instantly as a human or else to take birth on one of these other realms, perhaps later to be born on earth once again. When this view is present then death is not seen as the great catastrophe; it is not seen as the end but rather as a change. Even parting from loved ones is not seen as final, for there is the conviction that somewhere, at some time, they will meet again.

Other Faces of Death

Other faces of death are the bargaining face, the depressed face and the accepting face. A dying person wearing the bargaining face attempts to bargain with God or with beings from other realms by making promises like, 'I'll go on a pilgrimage to such and such a shrine provided you let me live.' Often there will be a promise added: 'I'll never ask another favour of you as long as you grant me this one.' When the dying person realises that bargaining has not worked he gets depressed, for now he can no longer deny the fact that he is seriously ill and is going to die.

The accepting face surfaces when the family and the dying person give in gladly to the realisation that death is going to take place. At this point much spiritual growth can take place.

An Apology

Before I go any further I would like to apologise to my father and to my brother and his girlfriend, should they ever hear this talk, for they may feel that it is too personal a story and therefore should not be told. However, in the teaching of spirituality it is noticeable that a story makes the strongest impact on people, no matter what their sex, age or educational background. Teaching linked to a story sinks more deeply into the mind of the listener than does dry theory which is not apparently linked to life. I know that for all of you the question of death and how to handle it will have more meaning and be more helpful if I link it to a real situation.

One person, I feel sure, will be very happy for me to tell this story and that is my mother herself, for she said to a friend of hers that if she ever recovered she would devote her life to helping people. Although she did not recover, the use of her story to illustrate the problems and possibility of spiritual growth in the death process goes some way towards fulfilling her wish to help others.

My Mother's Illness

Two years ago my mother got cancer. She had an operation to remove the cancerous growth, followed by radium treatment. She had the usual side-effects from this: loss of weight, vomiting and loss of energy. For a while she seemed to be on the road to recovery. She went back to work and returned to playing tennis, a game she loved dearly.

The first I heard of her approaching death was when I received a telephone call from my father in South Africa. He asked if I would go out to see my mother as her doctor had given her anything from two hours to two years to live. We had just started a residential meditation course, which I was teaching, so I booked to fly out to South Africa once the course was finished. As the week wore on and telephone calls flew back and forth it became clear that there was the possibility that she might not even last the week as her health was going downhill rapidly and she had stopped eating.

I sent her a mental message and told her not to die till I arrived at her bedside as I wished to see her before she left this realm. The date of departing for South Africa was brought forward to the last day of the course.

One thing my father did say during our first telephone conversation which made me think, 'Oh, dear', was that he had not told my mother that she was dying. Whichever way you look at it, not to face up to something is a negative move. Death is no exception to this rule.

The Face of Denial

If a family does not tell a relative that he is dying, the patient becomes psychologically isolated. Instead of there being a warm, open, close and tender relationship between the family and the dying person during those last few days of life, a falseness sets in, with everyone wearing a mask, pretending that everything will be all right, and that the person will get better and be off his sick bed in no time at all. There is a refusal to talk about what's happening in the moment and what the future holds. Rather is there a clinging to the past and to a fantasy of what everyone wishes to have happen.

In some cases, the person who has to break the bad news has a fear which he doesn't want to face. It is very difficult for many a doctor to tell a patient that he or she is dying. The doctor has taken the Hippocratic Oath to heal people, so when a patient dies on him it is the ultimate failure; he has not done his job properly. For this reason many a doctor would prefer to avoid the whole difficult issue of whether to tell or not to tell. The head of the family usually has the responsibility of informing the relative that he or she is dying but may choose not to, not out of consideration for the dying person but because he doesn't want to face his own feelings of embarrassment or distress. He doesn't want to face his distress at losing someone or the unpleasant feeling that will arise at the dying person's response to the news. Most people cover up the fact that they are more concerned about themselves than the dying person and rationalise away their discomfort by saying that it is best for the dying person if he does not know that death is imminent.

This is the 'denial' way of handling death. Far from comforting the dying person, it actually has the opposite effect; he feels isolated and lonely; excluded from a secret that the rest of the family shares. No longer is there honesty and openness between him and the rest of the family and because of the lack of truthfulness in the relationship, he feels he cannot express his feelings of anger, depression, or fear of what's going to happen to him once he dies. None of these things dare he bring out in the open to discuss and share with his family.

The conspiracy of silence does not allow the dying person to vent his anxieties through discussion. It does not allow him to receive any information about what happens after death. It does not allow him to receive advice from others as to how to die peacefully and with dignity. He cannot unburden himself and he cannot apologise for past errors towards family members. He cannot even say all the tender things he wishes he had said during his life but which his personality prevented him from saying; those things which are so much easier to say when you know that you are never going to see a person again. None of these things can be said because of the conspiracy of silence that the family has chosen to adopt.

The effect of denial on the family members who are left behind once death has occurred is equally negative. The shock of parting is greater and the grief at the loss is harder to cope with when ignore-ance has been chosen as the method of handling this particular difficult situation. Ignore-ance is a very negative thing and brings more trouble than comfort when it is used as a way of handling life's troubles.

Departure for South Africa
I had not been an active member of this South African family. I had not set foot in South Africa for fifteen years, I hadn't seen my brother for ten years, nor had I seen the house my parents currently occupied. Also, as we all lived so far apart from one another, there was never any question of frequent Sunday lunches together as a family unit. In short, I was somewhat on the outside of this particular family and because of that I felt I had no right to express my wants as to the way in which my mother's death should be approached. Before I even set foot on the plane, I had decided that if the family wished to handle my mother's death with the tools of denial, then I would go along with them and play the same game.

When I boarded the plane at Heathrow, I was not in the slightest bit concerned about how I'd cope with dying and death, for I knew that for me it would be easy. When you have spent the major part of your life dedicated to experiencing birth and death in the moment, there is no way that the death of your own or someone else's physical body is going to disturb you. What concerned me more was not the issue of dying but how to cook a meal.

Who was doing the cooking in my parents' home was never mentioned, but I had a sneaky feeling that the person who would end up doing the cooking was yours truly—and I hadn't done any cooking for four years. The knowledge of how to cook is like anything else, it's transient, as I had discovered last Christmas.

Christmas is the time when the Meditation Centre is empty of people other than Alan and myself, so it is one of the few occasions when we get to cook for ourselves, which we thoroughly enjoy. We decided on this occasion to cook rice as part of the midday menu but I soon discovered that I couldn't for the life of me remember how the rice should be done. I couldn't remember the quantity of rice to water or how long to cook it or whether one started with cold or hot water, and at that precise moment I had no access to a cookery book to look up the relevant information. I was somewhat startled at the discovery, especially as in the past I had been used to cooking a great deal, frequently for as many as seven people. Suddenly, I was like a raw beginner. The experience just underlined one of the major tenets of Buddhism which is that all things are transient—even cooking knowledge. When I stepped on to that plane I was really more concerned about cooking than the issue of dying.

On arrival at Jan Smuts Airport in Johannesburg my father was there to meet me and one of the first things he said was, 'You will be shocked at the sight of your mother.'

My mother looked like an Ethiopian famine victim, just skin and bones. I was told that a week ago she had weighed 30 kilograms (about 66 pounds) and that was when she was still eating. Now she was confined to bed, needing to be turned from her back to her side and back again every half an hour or so. She ate nothing, but she did have frequent sips of water and apple juice. Her lips were rubbed with lanolin to keep them moist and she was bathed in bed. That was the extent of the nursing she required. The rest was a waiting game. Waiting for her to die.

I watched relatives and friends go into her room. Some had seen her two weeks previously, some several months ago. Many came out crying. They were shocked at the sight of her, at how much she had physically deteriorated in the past few weeks. Many showed the face of anger. They were angry with the various doctors she had been to, for filling her with false hopes by telling her that she was going to recover. They were angry that she had not been told the true state of affairs. It was amazing how many were angry at her condition, feeling that the quality of her life was gone, that her body was spent and useless and that someone ought to do something about it and 'put her out of her misery'. Some were even angry with me for not having produced a grandchild for my mother, for they knew that she had dearly wished to have one.

Coping with the Angry Face
When the angry face of death presents itself it hits out at random, at anything and everything in sight. Anger is one of the stages in the dying process so, if you find yourself in this situation and are the object of someone's anger, don't be frightened or resist it. You help the other person to discharge his anger and thus his tension if you let him get cross with you and if you don't try to stand up for yourself or justify your position in any way. If you do stand up for yourself, or are silent but indignant, then you are resisting his anger and you don't help the other person one little bit. Anger cannot discharge if it is expressed only to be met with a brick wall of resistance. If you know that anger is a natural part of the reaction to the dying process then it is easier to accept it and not be disturbed by it.

Some of these friends said to me, 'You must have been so shocked to see your mother in this condition. It's so much better to be able to remember her the way she was, healthy, vital and able to move around. You must find it so distressing to watch her wasting away.' They found it very difficult to believe me when I said that I was neither shocked nor distressed. I was not shocked by the sight of my mother's wasted, stick-like body because I had been through this death experience before. When I was twenty-five I got married and shortly afterwards my husband became very ill. I nursed him during the illness with neither of us getting much sleep. He had to sit up at night to prevent his lungs from filling up with fluid and drowning him. I watched him getting thinner and thinner and when he eventually died he looked the way my mother looked, so I had come to associate dying with physical emaciation.

The other reason I was not shocked, but I did not mention this as it would have made my answer too complicated, is that when you have undergone a meditative training and you have absorbed the teaching so that it becomes part of you, then your responses to many of life's events are quite different to other people's. With the training you gradually learn to let go of the past, and not to drag it into the present moment to destroy what you find there.

When I saw my mother for the first time after I stepped off the plane there was immediate acceptance of the way she was, with her thin, worn-out body. There was no comparison with the way she looked the last time I saw her when she was well, healthy and mobile. Because there was no comparison, there was no thinking, 'Oh, doesn't she look awful. I wish she looked well and healthy again.' When you don't drag forward into the present moment the memory of the way the person used to look, then there is no problem. There can only be distress in the mind when there is expectation; if you expect the person to be the way he used to be. If you then cling to that expectation, and you *want* the individual to be the way he was, that clinging to the past will give you awful problems. You will find yourself crying, depressed and suffering deeply.

135

The Hospice Movement

Something which did delight me when I arrived at my mother's bedside was to discover that the face of denial was no longer being exercised by the family. This change had been brought about because my mother had called in the Hospice movement.

The Hospice movement exists in many countries in the world and deals exclusively with the terminally ill. I can only tell you about the Hospice movement as I was exposed to it, although I assume it functions in more or less the same manner in whatever country it is found. Its aim is to get dying people to face up to their situation and to their own feelings about death. In that way, the dying person's preparation for death is such that not only does he grow spiritually in those last days of life but also he dies with dignity. The family looking on also benefits from the presence of the Hospice movement for they too are encouraged to come to terms with their own feelings about death and dying. Those feelings particularly include the grief associated with the tragedy that has suddenly hit the family as well as the grief at the forthcoming loss of the loved one. By facing up to these feelings much of the grief is discharged before the person dies, thus making the death, the funeral and the subsequent loneliness easier to handle.

The undertaker said that the moment he walks into a house just a few hours after the death, he can tell if the people from the Hospice movement have been involved because the dead person's family is so much calmer than in households where they have not been called in. I think they are a wonderful group of people, doing much valuable work, and would unhesitatingly recommend them in any case involving terminal illness.

The Hospice allocates one nursing sister to look after the physical requirements of the dying person and one person, whom they call a care-giver, to look after the emotional needs of both the dying person and the family. These two visit the home once or twice a day right up to the day of death. The care-giver spends much time listening and talking with the dying person and the various family members. Dying is, after all, a family affair for most people. It doesn't affect only the person who is dying; it also affects the husband or wife who's left behind, as well as their children. All the remaining members of the family have to come to terms with the illness, the bereavement and subsequent changes in life-style and relationships.

I discovered that the Hospice's attitude to dying and death is identical to the Buddhist attitude. They encourage awareness of the situation and a non-judgemental attitude so that, whichever face of death is presented, it is not denied but rather is accepted and worked with so that, in the best case, both the dying person and the family arrive at the face of acceptance. Only when there is total acceptance is there the possibility of the positive qualities of love and peacefulness being able to flow and when those are there, the person is able to die knowing they have grown in understanding from their illness and from facing death.

The accepting face of death allows the person to view the whole experience as worthwhile, because so much is gained, rather than seeing death as a waste and a failure, to be done quietly in a corner out of sight of the world. He doesn't 'go out' fighting against the inevitable, terrified and enraged at death. On the contrary, he dies with the mind settled, knowing that both he and the family have gained something from the experience. This is dying with dignity.

The care-giver allocated to my mother believed that death was not the end, which meant that I could happily talk to my mother about what would happen to her after death without cutting across the Hospice message.

The Last Days

My mother became bedridden during the last two weeks of her life. During the first week the family turned her from her side to her back to her side again, to relieve the stiffness and the discomfort of lying in one position, but once that first week had passed, the accumulative effect of days and days without food meant that the muscles that usually pad the bones and make it comfortable for us to lie on our sides had wasted away. Anybody touching her body and moving it, even slightly, caused her great pain and her face would screw up with agony so, from this point on, she lay on her back day and night.

From time to time we gave her a teaspoon of water or apple juice. She could no longer suck the water through a straw for herself as she had been doing for the past week, so we would lift her head up and carefully pour the water into her mouth. From time to time we cleaned her teeth and tongue, put lanolin on her lips and sponged her face with a damp facecloth. Other than this we could do nothing more for her physically.

She lay hour after hour on her back, conscious most of the time. The nursing sister had provided morphine to control the physical pain and a sedative to relax her body and help her sleep. Both these drugs, but particularly the morphine, knocked her unconscious, sometimes for as long as nine hours at a time. As the days passed she refused the medication, which was normally given to her every four hours. Not taking any medication, she was conscious for much of the day and night. She lay there hour after hour, letting out little moans from time to time, and saying that this waiting to die was terrible; it was the worst possible torture.

During those two bedridden weeks she wasn't in much physical pain but she most definitely was in mental pain. The mental pain was caused by her inability to accept the waiting period and her inability to see any purpose in it. My father also suffered, for he too could not see any purpose to her lying there, just waiting to die. Her body was spent; it was now useless. To him it appeared that she was just marking time, waiting to be released from a useless experience. He said that if he could see any point at all to her lying there, if she were gaining something, then he would be all for it but as he could not see that she could possibly get anything out of it, he thought the whole thing was tragic. At times he got quite angry about it. Friends got angry about it. My mother herself would get angry and then depressed. These two faces of death, the angry face and the depressed face, showed up often during that final week. They didn't last long but they were there as frequent visitors.

My mother was a Westerner with a Westerner's conditioning which says one should be a productive member of society. To lie in bed day in and day out, not being able to cook and care for others, not being able to go to work, is unproductive and so waiting to die is seen as a complete waste of time and produces lots of guilt feelings for the average Westerner. From a very early age we are taught that we must show some concrete physical results for our existence if we are to be regarded as worthwhile human beings. It is common for Western parents to say to their children, 'Don't just sit there doing nothing. Do something useful with your time.' Given this conditioning it is natural that lying in bed waiting to die will be seen by both patient and onlookers as 'doing nothing'. At least if you are actually dying that is doing *something*.

Waiting for Death
What's the point of all this waiting, all this suffering? Unless they have already sorted out their views on the purpose of life, this question obsesses the dying person, the family, the friends and the medical people involved with the patient at this time. If there is little spiritual development, this is the point at which much suffering is encountered. There is mental turmoil about the best course of action. This is when discussion about euthanasia occurs. This is when the nurse who has access to drugs is often pressurised by the patient or the family or both to give the patient something which will end his life. This is the point where if you do not have a clear view about the disadvantages of killing, the true purpose of life and what happens after death, you may well find that

you are one of those people pressurising the nurse to take the patient's life. There is so much emotion in the air at this time that to start sorting out your views about life and death is an impossibility; your already-existing belief system simply takes over.

In contrast, for those steeped in spirituality there is no suffering; there is a total acceptance of the situation. You know why there is a waiting period. There is no resistance to waiting. You see it as a beautiful time and not as a tragic one.

There is a purpose in this waiting for death, and there is a purpose in it for the members of the family who also wait, helpless to do anything other than tend to the dying person's occasional physical needs. The point of the waiting period is closely linked with the whole purpose of life.

We visit this human realm for the purpose of learning how to experience joy or pain without judgement; we have to learn to accept fully any experience and to let it go when it's finished.

At first we have a very strong tendency to seek out pleasure and reject all that is painful or in any way unpleasant. We will return time and time again to this human realm until we have learnt the lesson of acceptance of all the opposites of joy and sadness, praise and blame, illness and health, waiting and action, anger and peacefulness, life and death. Waiting to die or waiting for a loved one to die is to experience one of these opposites—one of the unpleasant opposites. If the dying person in particular can be patient and accept the wait, knowing that death will visit when the time and conditions are right, then he can make great strides forward in his spiritual evolution. It is never too late to learn.

Teachings about Death
Each day I spent time with my mother, either talking to her or just sitting there meditating. I talked to her about what would happen to her after she died. I talked to her about

how to die, which is just to let go; to let go of life. She had at one stage asked the Hospice nurse to give her a pill to make her die and when it was refused, she asked the care-giver how to die. The care-giver's answer was the same as the Buddhist one: just let go. After receiving this advice my mother asked me if I would help her to die. I said I would. However, all I could do was to assist in providing suitable mental conditions so that she would find herself more capable of letting go. *She* had to do the letting go; I couldn't do it for her.

I taught her the meditation on loving kindness as well as some visualisation meditations, one of which was to visualise herself letting go of life. The loving kindness was to help achieve a relaxed mental state from which letting go is easier to accomplish. I talked to her about how dying was like going to sleep at night; when you wake up the next day you are different and yet still the same. Dying is like going to sleep and waking in a different place from where you went to sleep; you will find you are different and yet the same. One of the differences is that you will have a different body; a body which is free from disease and free from pain.

I told her there was no need to fear dying. She didn't fear going to sleep at night and yet when she went to sleep she ventured into the unknown, for she didn't know if she would wake up again. She didn't know if she would sleep well or badly or whether she would dream. She could dream and find it nightmarish. She did not know what lay ahead when she put her head down on the pillow and closed her eyes, and yet she was quite happy to do it and she was not afraid of letting go of consciousness. So it should be with dying. It is just like going to sleep.

I told her what would happen once she had let go of life. She would wake up in a fully-formed mental body. Passing through death's door is like the moment of birth; there would be people present who would be delighted to see her and who would want to assist her in her new life. Just as there are relatives round a new-born baby who are thrilled at the new arrival, so there are beings around the deceased to welcome them into their new life.

Being Willing to Die

Someone I met in South Africa who was training with the Hospice movement to become a care-giver told me how she had mentioned to a nursing sister that death was not the end; that there were more lives to come. It seems that the sister was absolutely horrified at the idea of continuous life. She said she could think of nothing worse than coming back again and again, which seems to imply that the idea of rebirth rather than being comforting is, for some people, a distressing concept.

However, even the individual who thinks the idea of rebirth to be horrific or silly is very willing to entertain the idea of returning to the human realm when faced with the immediate prospect of *his own* life coming to an end. My mother was one such type. Many years ago I had mentioned the subject of rebirth to her and she was horrified. She said the last thing in the world she wanted was to come back again. On her deathbed, when the end of life was a reality and not just something that lay off in the remote future, then she was only too happy to hear about rebirth.

The same observation can be made of the person who begs those closest to him to give him a pill or some poison or in some way to end his life. It looks as if he wants life to cease, but what he really wants is for the *physical and mental pain* to cease; he does not want *life* to cease. This was clearly the case for my mother. She begged for a pill to end her life and yet she clung on desperately, taking a whole week from the time she asked for the pill until the time she let go of life.

One of the major conditions bringing about death is the mental letting go of life. It was noticeable that my mother's actions contradicted her words. She wanted life but she did not want the unpleasantness of a sick body, which is totally understandable; that is what we all want. We all want life but we don't want suffering, either of a physical or mental nature.

I told her constantly that death would occur when the conditions were right and not to panic and think she was going to last in this ill state forever; that everything that is born must come to an end. That is the Law. The illness had a beginning, therefore it would come to an end. I spoke much on this subject to try and calm down her distress at lying there waiting to die.

The Agony of Waiting

If you want to know what distress at waiting is like for the dying person, take a look at a very familiar meditative experience. You're sitting doing an hour's meditation and your back starts to hurt. Do you just note that the pain exists, let it go, and pass on to the next object, which would be the *right* and *dignified* way of handling back pain? Or do you start to get agitated, wondering how long the hour has to go, wondering if you can bear to sit there any longer, wondering if you'll jump up and rush out of the room?

The instruction is that you must finish the hour regardless of the trials and tribulations which beset you and, furthermore, that you mustn't move to ease the back pain, for that would imply an attempt to avoid the pain instead of accepting it. You sit there in great distress, willing the hour to end, getting more and more tense and wondering if you can handle any more of this mental distress. This response to the unpleasant experience of back pain is no different from the response to waiting to die. The way the mind works is identical in both cases. In both situations the person wants to get away from something he finds unpleasant. The 'wanting to get away' is the mental factor of hatred and wherever there is hatred there is suffering. The meditative training is to stop the mind from wanting to get away. When you can do that, distress ceases.

Every meditator here has experienced wanting to get away from a painful hour of practice so, when faced with someone wanting to get away from the agony of waiting to die, you can understand and sympathise fully with him or her. You know from your own experience how difficult and frustrating is the handling of the desire to get away from something unpleasant. With the back pain you had the remedy for the ceasing of distress at your fingertips: all you had to do was to let go of your want for something other, but *still* you found it difficult to put the remedy into practice. How much more difficult is it for the person who is dying who has not been practising how to let go? You know what he is going through and can sympathise with him. This will help you to find the right words to assist the dying person to cope with his agony.

Happiness in the Face of Death

I talked to my mother about how desirable it was to die with the mind happy or tranquil. To help her accomplish this I taught her and often guided her through a visualisation of tranquillity and happiness. Thinking of a happy time in the past immediately gladdens the mind and if you constantly re-visualise it, in no time at all your mind will be filled with happiness.

I told her to remember a happy or tranquil scene. As an example of what I meant, I reminded her that the night before the whole family had been sitting round her bed, joking and laughing, and when I had looked at her I noticed that she was really enjoying the occasion and that she too was laughing at the jokes. I thought that the memory of the family together, laughing and united, would be something she would treasure. A little while after this she lapsed into sleep.

When she awoke, she started talking about Brassknocker Hill, which is in Wiltshire, not far from the Meditation Centre. As you come down the hill, magnificent views of the English countryside are spread out before you. There are hills and trees, a river and many fields containing grazing sheep and cows. She said that was what she had chosen to visualise. I should have realised she would want to choose a scene like that because she loved nature and animals and had dearly wanted to spend her last days in Britain. That scene contained many of her major loves: it contained countryside and animals, it was tranquil and it was in Britain. She spent a lot of time after that visualising the beauty and tranquillity of Brassknocker Hill.

When sitting silently with her I always did loving kindness meditation (*mettā*), exclusively towards her, to assist her to relax. If she could relax sufficiently then she could withdraw her attention from the world about her and so enter the first stage of death. She desperately wanted to die. She wasn't frightened of dying, but being alive and waiting for the end to come was too much.

The Goodbye Ceremony

After I had been in South Africa for two days the family went through the 'goodbye' ceremony. This is one of the Hospice's methods of helping the person to die. When the individual decides that he is ready and that he wants to die then the Hospice care-giver advises the family to assemble and one by one to go into the dying person's room to spend some time talking with him about personal things. A member of the family may want to say loving words which up to that moment he or she has been too embarrassed or too self-conscious to mention, or maybe want to apologise for past actions. It is an occasion for opening up and letting go of the defences and for saying all the things one may have neglected to say. It is a time to profess one's love for the person, it's a time to say thank you to the person for having been part of one's life, it's a time to say goodbye.

It was a Sunday morning when this happened to us. My father went in, I went in, my uncle went in, and my father went to fetch my brother from the tennis court where he was playing a league match so that he could come and say his goodbyes. For the rest of that day we sat and waited. Evidently once the goodbyes have been said and provided everything which should have been said is said, then death follows very shortly afterwards, sometimes as quickly as two hours later.

I wondered if my mother would manage to let go that quickly. Letting go is not so easy. This I knew from spending year upon year listening to meditation reports. Even when a meditator can see clearly that his present state of distress is caused by himself to himself, by clinging on to physical or mental pain, he still cannot let go of the pain. This is when the meditation teacher hears the cry, 'I *know* I'm doing it to myself, but I just can't seem to stop it!' Even though the meditator dearly wants to rid himself of suffering and knows of the remedy—to let go—still he is incapable of relaxing his grip on suffering.

The family waited all day Sunday. Monday we were still waiting. Tuesday we were still waiting. Seven days later we were still waiting. She was like so many other human beings, she couldn't let go even though she dearly wished to. It's hard to let go. It's even hard to let go of the things we hate. It takes much meditative training to learn to let go.

Mother caused the family many a chuckle. After that Sunday when we all said goodbye, a little ritual used to be performed on many of the evenings following. Mother used to announce that she was going to die now, and she would call us all in to be with her at her death moment. On one occasion she said, 'Oh, this waiting takes so long I think I'll go out and get drunk whilst I wait.' It was such a funny statement coming from someone so thin, so immobile, so incapable of moving her limbs. She couldn't even lift a glass of water to her face, let alone a glass of alcohol.

On another occasion she called us to her bedside and said, 'I'm going now. I haven't died before so I can't be certain that this is it, but I think it is.' Again the family chuckled. I asked her why she thought she was dying. She said because she couldn't remember anything. As she had just taken some morphine and a sedative, I came to the conclusion that these two drugs had so affected her mind that she had temporarily lost her memory. This was such an unfamiliar state to her that she thought it was a sign of approaching death. Needless to say she didn't die on that occasion either.

Disengaging from Daily Life

During the last week of my mother's life the family decided to take it in turns to sit with her during the night to attend to her physical needs whenever she awoke. My brother and his girlfriend sat with her from 10pm to midnight, my father from midnight to 3am, and I sat with her from 3 to 6am. On some days a nurse would arrive at 7am, otherwise my father and I looked after her during the day as well.

We organised the shift system because we felt it was very tiring for my father to be doing the nursing all night with no assistance from anyone else and it would have been a very distressing experience for him had he fallen asleep next to my mother and then awoken to find that she had been dead for several hours, that rigor mortis had set in and that the body fluids had started to leak out from all the orifices.

When the dying person is getting near the end it is not always appropriate to visit him because it pulls his awareness back into the physical realm and delays the dying process. In order to die a person has to become uninterested in what is going on around him. He has to become 'disengaged', which is a term favoured by the Hospice movement. In short, he has to let go of his involvement with the physical world. This is the first stage in the dying process.

It had become clear very early on that my mother was far too involved with the world for death to occur. Whenever there were three or four of us gathered in the house and a meal time approached, she would want to know from my father if we were all being cared for and if he was collecting the spring onions and tomatoes and green peppers from the garden to be used in the salads. She would tell him that if he didn't use the vegetables they would go rotten.

147

When someone rang the front doorbell at night, she would want to know who it was and why they were there. One day, at 3am, there was a tremendous commotion outside the house. My mother wanted to know what it was. I told her it was cats fighting. 'Ah,' she said, 'I've heard dogs and chickens too.' All this showed too much interest in what was going on around her.

Have you ever had the experience when ill of being so uninterested in what is going on around you that you are quite sure that even if the whole house fell down around your sick bed, you wouldn't care less? You're sure you wouldn't even be bothered to investigate, but would just lie there. That is being uninvolved with the world around you; that is being disengaged from the physical universe.

Exactly the same disengagement has to occur for those meditators who practise concentration meditation and who wish to enter the deeply internalised calmness called *jhāna*. In order to get deeply concentrated they withdraw their interest from the physical senses and from thinking for long periods. Occasionally a sound does impinge; maybe a telephone rings. The ringing seems very far away and muffled, and the meditator feels no inclination whatsoever to get up and answer the phone. This state of indifference is reflected in the meditator's thoughts: there is either a complete absence of thinking or there is an occasional thought concerned with the immediate present or with the state the meditator is attempting to achieve. If thoughts arise about organising the house or the business or the garden, then the meditator is too involved in the physical universe and is not sufficiently disengaged to enter *jhāna*.

In order to get deeply concentrated or to die, the same disengaged state has to be entered into.

The Death
On the morning of the day my mother died I was standing in the kitchen talking to a friend of my parents who had come in to arrange flowers around the house. We were talking in

normal voices but a message came via my father from my mother. Please would we talk more quietly. It was a very good sign. It meant that she was starting to let go of the physical realm.

In the early hours of the Tuesday morning, nine days after I had arrived in South Africa, I got out of bed and dressed ready to start my allotted 3am shift. When I entered my parents' room I saw tissues piled high on the side of the bed. My father had put them there so that whoever nursed my mother could wipe away the froth of phlegm from her lips. This build-up of phlegm was something new and it had started only an hour or so before.

My mother could no longer swallow the phlegm that gathered in her throat, so she pushed it out of her mouth where it formed in a froth around her lips. I had to be alert to quickly wipe it away or it disappeared into her mouth again.

After I had sat with her for a while it became obvious that she was getting into a state of panic about choking on the phlegm. I put my hands over hers and told her not to panic about choking. I told her that choking was the way her physical body was going to die. I told her that she had another body, a new one that was not subject to illness and physical discomfort and which was young and vibrant. I told her that she should let go of this worn-out body and get into her new body and that if she found it difficult to let go of her diseased body, not to worry, for she would suddenly find herself in her new body ready to go on her journey. I told her that she would then have a long, well-earned rest, after which she could decide where she wanted to go.

Whilst I was talking to her she had turned her head to one side so that her ear was directly in line with my mouth. When I finished speaking, she settled right down. The atmosphere went calm. She stopped spitting out the phlegm. She stopped groaning. The mental atmosphere went calmer still. She let the phlegm start to choke her. There was one death rattle. (The death rattle is a fairly loud guttural, gurgling sound created by choking on phlegm.) There were a few moments' silence. Then another death rattle.

I started to speak again. I told her she was doing very well. I told her to continue to let go. I told her that once she was out of her physical body and in her new body she would find herself up near the ceiling looking down on her old body and on me sitting in the chair beside her. I told her not to fear leaving her old body, that it was like moving from an old house to a new one. My mother loved moving house. She and my father rarely stayed in a house for more than five years. After three or four years she would get itchy feet and start off on the house-hunt once again. I reminded her how much she loved moving into a new and different house and that leaving her body was like leaving an old house and moving into a new one.

A few seconds after that she died.

Her face had gone ashen white. I'd been told by the Hospice people that it would. All day the family had watched this ashen colour gradually creeping up her face, starting with her chin. By evening it had reached her eyes. By the time she died it had covered her whole face.

Once she had died, I was thrilled that she had made it. She had tried so hard all week to let go and at last had mastered the technique. Knowing that she would still be around but in mental body now, I congratulated her, told her I loved her, thanked her for being my mother, said goodbye, and wished her well in her new life. I told her I would go and fetch the rest of the family so that they too could say their final goodbyes.

Learning how to die properly is all about learning how to let go, learning how to watch the natural ebb and flow of all things, learning that life is a process of continual beginnings and endings, continual birth and death. When you see this cyclical movement clearly then there is no more fear of death. When you have learnt *that* not only have you learnt how to die but you have also learnt how to live.

150

A Meditation Retreat

Alan & Jacqui James

Alan and Jacqui James have been teaching insight (*vipassanā*) meditation, the pragmatic, experiential side of the Buddhist philosophy, for over fifteen years, and this book provides a selection of the talks they have given to their students at their Meditation Centre, The House of Inner Tranquillity, in Wiltshire. With a clarity and directness of approach that can only come from understanding, they cover such topics as how to meditate, hindrances to the practice and how to overcome them, the relationship between meditation teacher and student, and enlightenment itself—the ultimate goal of the spiritual journey.

While many of these talks were especially designed for the new meditator embarking on his/her first retreat, they will all provide inspiration and a wealth of wisdom for novice and experienced meditator alike, for anyone in fact who has ever felt, 'There *must* be more to life than this!'

172 *pages* 13 *black & white photographs*
216×130*mm* ISBN 0 9511769 0 0 *paperback* £6.50 *inc p&p*

Copies of
Modern Buddhism and A Meditation Retreat
available from

England: Aukana Publishing
Ardgay House
Middlehill
Box
Wiltshire
SN14 9QD

Modern Buddhism   £7.50 inc p&p
A Meditation Retreat   £6.50 inc p&p

For information on insight meditation classes in the Wiltshire area, write to Jacqui and Alan James, c/o Aukana Publishing at the above address.

Canada: Paul MacRae
14 Cluny Drive
Toronto
M4V 2P7

Modern Buddhism $18.00 inc p&p
A Meditation Retreat $16.00 inc p&p

For information on insight meditation classes in the Toronto area, write to Paul MacRae at the above address.

Australia: Mrs D.W. Tranter
Australian Broadcasting Corporation
Radio News Room
T.V. Building
600 Coronation Drive
Toowong
Brisbane
Q 4066

Modern Buddhism $17.00 inc p&p
A Meditation Retreat $15.00 inc p&p
